THE KING AND I

BARBARA ANN MARY MACK

© 2022 BARBARA ANN MARY MACK. ALL RIGHTS RESERVED.

NO PART OF THIS BOOK MAY BE REPRODUCED, STORED IN
A RETRIEVAL SYSTEM, OR TRANSMITTED BY ANY MEANS
WITHOUT THE WRITTEN PERMISSION OF THE AUTHOR.

AUTHORHOUSE™
1663 LIBERTY DRIVE
BLOOMINGTON, IN 47403
WWW.AUTHORHOUSE.COM
PHONE: 833-262-8899

BECAUSE OF THE DYNAMIC NATURE OF THE INTERNET, ANY WEB ADDRESSES OR LINKS CONTAINED IN THIS BOOK MAY HAVE CHANGED SINCE PUBLICATION AND MAY NO LONGER BE VALID. THE VIEWS EXPRESSED IN THIS WORK ARE SOLELY THOSE OF THE AUTHOR AND DO NOT NECESSARILY REFLECT THE VIEWS OF THE PUBLISHER, AND THE PUBLISHER HEREBY DISCLAIMS ANY RESPONSIBILITY FOR THEM.

ANY PEOPLE DEPICTED IN STOCK IMAGERY PROVIDED BY GETTY IMAGES ARE MODELS,
AND SUCH IMAGES ARE BEING USED FOR ILLUSTRATIVE PURPOSES ONLY.
CERTAIN STOCK IMAGERY © GETTY IMAGES.

THIS BOOK IS PRINTED ON ACID-FREE PAPER.

ISBN: 978-1-6655-4759-8 (SC)
ISBN: 978-1-6655-4758-1 (HC)
ISBN: 978-1-6655-4760-4 (E)

PRINT INFORMATION AVAILABLE ON THE LAST PAGE.

PUBLISHED BY AUTHORHOUSE 01/07/2021

authorHOUSE

BEHOLD MY PRESENT TESTAMENT: THE CONTINUANCE OF MY OLD AND NEW TESTAMENTS, *SAYS THE LORD JESUS*

"VOLUME SIXTY THREE"

"THE KING AND I"

BY:

BARBARA ANN MARY MACK

BEGAN: NOVEMBER 12, 2021

COMPLETED: DECEMBER 7, 2021

Barbara Ann Mary Mack

April 7, 2024

TABLE OF CONTENTS

THE KING *HAS RETURNED* VII

DEDICATION IX

ACKNOWLEDGMENT XI

ABOUT *THE AUTHOR* XIII

ABOUT *THE BOOK* XV

MY OTHER PUBLISHED BOOKS 181

THE KING *HAS RETURNED*

KING *JESUS* SPEAKING TO EARTH'S INHABITANTS TODAY

I HAVE RETURNED, YOU SEE-
TO REVEAL THE HOLY PRESENCE OF *THE HEAVEN SENT KING ALMIGHTY.*
I HAVE RETURNED THROUGH *MY SERVANT AND MESSENGER.*
YES, DEAR CHILDREN! *I HAVE RETURNED THROUGH BARBARA, MY OBEDIENT DAUGHTER.*
FOR SHE HAS BEEN *PURIFIED AND MADE HOLY.*
YES, DEAR ONES! *BARBARA HAS BEEN PURIFIED BY ETERNAL ME.*
SHE WALKS ACCORDING TO *MY HOLY COMMANDS-*
FOR HER OBEDIENT SOUL *IS IN MY HOLY HANDS, SAYS KING JESUS*

DEDICATION

TO ALMIGHTY GOD; THE LORD *JESUS, THE GREAT AND HOLY KING OF KINGS*

ACKNOWLEDGMENT

THROUGH DIVINE REVELATION FROM ALMIGHTY GOD, THE GREAT AND HOLY KING, I BOW IN THE PRESENCE OF HIS EXISTENCE EVERY DAY

BARBARA ANN MARY MACK

ABOUT *THE AUTHOR*

As a humbled servant of Almighty God, the Great and Holy King, I proceed in the divine work that He has commissioned me to do every day.

Barbara Ann Mary Mack is the God sent and chosen author of *Fifty* previously published God dictated books. She has been a deliverer of God's Holy Words and messages for over twenty years. Barbara has one daughter and one granddaughter, who have accompanied her on her missionary work for the Lord God over the years. Barbara presently resides in Philadelphia, PA.

ABOUT *THE BOOK*

THE KING AND I CONSISTS OF MANY CURRENT SPIRITUAL SAYINGS BETWEEN CHRIST *JESUS*, THE HEAVEN SENT KING, AND BARBARA ANN MARY MACK, HIS SENT MESSENGER AND PROPHETESS

INTRODUCING CHRIST JESUS, THE FOREVER REIGNING AND RULING KING

CHRIST JESUS SPEAKING

DEAR CHILDREN-
OH, MY BLESSED ONES FROM EVERY EARTHLY AND HEAVENLY NATION.

I, THE GREAT AND HOLY ETERNAL KING, AM IN THE MIDST OF MY EARTHLY LOVED ONES TODAY.

I HAVE RETURNED IN YOUR MIDST, SO THAT I MAY LEAD THOSE WHOM I HAVE CHOSEN BEFORE THE REALM OF TIME, TO FOLLOW THE KING'S LIFE SAVING AND REWARDING HOLY WAY.

DEAR CHILDREN: DEAR SISTER AND BROTHER-
BELIEVE ME, CHRIST, THE FOREVER-LIVING KING, THAT THERE IS NO OTHER.

THERE ARE NO OTHER WAYS-
THAT CAN SAVE YOUR WANDERING SOULS DURING THESE PANDEMIC DAYS.

OUT OF GREAT UNCHANGING LOVE-
GOD, OUR HEAVENLY FATHER, HAS SENT ME, YOUR DIVINE KING FROM SWEET HEAVEN ABOVE.

THERE IS NO OTHER-
WHO CAN *SAVE THE CHILDREN OF GOD, OUR FATHER.*

HEED MY HEAVENLY WARNING-
FOR NOW, YOU ARE IN THE HOLY PRESENCE OF *CHRIST JESUS, THE FORETOLD LIFE SAVING KING.*

COME TO ME, *O BLESSED ONES-*
DO NOT FIGHT AGAINST *THE HEAVENLY KING WHO HAS COME FOR HIS BLESSED EARTHLY DAUGHTERS AND SONS.*

COME! COME! COME!
ENTER, O BLESSED ONES, INTO MY EARTHLY KINGDOM!

COME TO ME, *SAYS KING JESUS*

KING *JESUS* SPEAKING

O BLESSED ONES!
O CHOSEN DAUGHTERS AND SONS-

COME WITH ME-
ENTER THE THRONE OF KING JESUS; THE ALMIGHTY!

COME TO MY THRONE TODAY-
ENTER MY REALM, WHICH *LEADS TO MY LIFE SAVING ONLY WAY.*

FOR *ONLY YOU-*
CAN FOLLOW *THE VOICE OF THE KING, WHO IS HOLY, ETERNAL AND TRUE.*

YOU HAVE BEEN CHOSEN-
YOU ARE MY BLESSED AND BELOVED CHILDREN.

FOR YOU HAVE *FOLLOWED ME FAITHFULLY-*
THEREFORE, YOU WILL NOW WITNESS *THE THRONE OF CHRIST JESUS, THE FOREVER-REIGNING KING ALMIGHTY.*

YOU WILL *WITNESS-*
THE DEPTH AND FULLNESS OF *MY GLORY AND HOLINESS.*

You are *my blessed ones.*
You are *my worthy daughters and sons.*

You have been *chosen, you see-*
to live throughout sweet eternity with your *great and holy King Almighty.*

Come! Come! Come!
Enter, my lovely children, into my everlasting kingdom!

For *holy and true-*
is the heavenly King who has blessed all of you.

Come! Come! *Come unto me!*
Come, O beautiful children of *the forever-living Christ Almighty!!!*

THE KING AND I HAVE COME FOR YOU

BARBARA SPEAKING

WE HAVE COME FOR YOU, *DEAR BROTHER*.
WE HAVE COME FOR YOU, *O BLESSED DAUGHTER*.
FOR WE HAVE BEEN SENT BY *THE DIVINE POWER AND PRESENCE OF GOD, OUR HEAVENLY FATHER*.

FOR *HE IS A FATHER WHO DOES CARE*.
AND HE WANTS HIS EARTHLY CHILDREN TO KNOW THAT *HE IS NEAR*.

HE HAS SENT US-
HE HAS SENT HIS MESSENGER, BARBARA, AND OUR *SAVIOR, CHRIST JESUS.*

GET UP, DEAR BROTHER!
GET UP, DEAR SISTER!
COME AND GREET THE FAITHFUL ONES (KING JESUS AND BARBARA), WHO WERE SENT BY ALMIGHTY GOD, OUR HEAVENLY FATHER!

FOR *WE HAVE COME, YOU SEE-*
TO RESCUE *THOSE WHO WERE CHOSEN BY THE FATHER ALMIGHTY*.

FOR *HOLY AND TRUE-*
IS THE HEAVENLY FATHER WHO LOVES YOU.

JESUS, OUR HEAVEN SENT KING, HAS ARRIVED:
WHAT WILL YOU DO?

<u>BARBARA SPEAKING</u>

CHRIST, THE FORETOLD KING, HAS ARRIVED, YOU SEE-
AND NOW, *EARTH IS IN THE HOLY PRESENCE OF THE KING ALMIGHTY.*

HE HAS ARRIVED, AND *HE IS IN OUR MIDST.*
BEHOLD, O EARTH'S RESIDENTS, *CHRIST, THE EVERLASTING KING, DOES EXIST!!!*

WHAT WILL YOU DO NOW, *DEAR ONES?*
WHAT WILL YOU DO, *O NEEDY DAUGHTERS AND SONS?*

YOU ARE IN *THE KING'S HOLY PRESENCE-*
COME OUT! COME OUT! *COME OUT OF YOUR SHELTERED RESIDENCE!*

FOR *CHRIST, THE HEAVEN SENT KING, YOU SEE-*
HAS COME TO *REVEAL HIS HEAVENLY DIVINITY.*

COME OUT OF *YOUR CAPTIVITY!*
COME OUT AND *GET A GLIMPSE OF THE KING'S GLORY!*

FOR *CHRIST JESUS, YOU SEE-*
HAS COME BACK TO *FREE YOU AND ME.*

COME, DEAR CAPTIVE BROTHER!
COME, DEAR CAPTIVE SISTER!
COME, ALL YOU LANDS, AND GET A TASTE OF *THE HEAVEN SENT KING, FOR HE IS OUR CREATOR AND FATHER!!!*

BEHOLD! BEHOLD! BEHOLD!
FOR HE COMES WITH *HIS HEAVENLY WORDS OF GOLD!*

OBSERVE *HIS HOLY EXISTENCE-*
REJOICE, AS *HE ENTERS YOUR EARTHLY RESIDENCE!*

FOR *CHRIST, THE FOREVER-LIVING KING, YOU SEE-*
HAS COME BACK TO *RESCUE YOU AND ME!!!*

IF YOU WOULD ONLY *COME TO THE KING*

CHRIST *JESUS,* THE FOREVER-LIVING KING, SPEAKING

DEAR SWEET CHILDREN-
YES! *MY BELOVED ONES FROM EVERY NATION.*

IF YOU WOULD SURRENDER AND *COME TO CHRIST, THE FOREVER-LIVING KING-*
I WILL TAKE YOU TO A LEVEL IN THIS LIFE THAT WOULD *REVEAL TO YOU MY GREAT AND HOLY THING.*

FOR *KNOWING ME, DEAR ONES-*
ALLOW YOU TO *ENTER INTO A LIFE OF GOODNESS THAT I HAVE WAITING FOR MY OBEDIENT DAUGHTERS AND SONS.*

IF YOU COME TO ME-
I WILL SHOW YOU THE BENEFICIAL THINGS THAT WOULD PERMIT YOU TO WITNESS THE BEAUTY OF OUR ORIGIN AND FATHER, JEHOVAH GOD ALMIGHTY.

THROUGH ME-
YOU WILL BE PERMITTED TO ENTER THE HOLY GATES THAT LEAD TO THE HOME OF OUR GOD AND FATHER; SWEET ETERNITY.

FOR I AM THE OPEN GATE, YOU SEE-
THAT LEADS TO THE MIGHTY THRONE OF GOD ALMIGHTY.

FOR HOLY AND TRUE-
IS THE GOD AND HEAVENLY FATHER WHO FORMED BLESSED YOU.

HOLY, HOLY, HOLY-
IS OUR GOD AND FATHER, JEHOVAH, THE ALMIGHTY!!!

WHEN YOU COME TO THE KING

<u>*CHRIST JESUS, THE FOREVER-LIVING KING SPEAKING*</u>

DEAR CHILDREN-
YOU ARE MY FAITHFUL AND CHOSEN.

WHEN YOU COME TO ME-
I WILL SHOW YOU EVERYTHING THAT BELONGS TO GOD ALMIGHTY.

FOR, MY EXISTENCE-
HAS PLACED YOU IN MY HOLY PRESENCE.

When you come to Me-
I will permit you to experience a life that is full of grace for those whom I have set free.

Come! Come! Come unto Me-
Enter the holy gates that lead to the throne of your everlasting King Almighty.

For holy and true-
is the King who has summoned and called blessed you.

The KING will deliver you

Christ JESUS, the forever-living KING speaking

I will deliver you, dear ones-
from the sin and pain that have captured My weak and vulnerable daughters and sons.

I will deliver you-
from the realm of destruction, as you enter the gates that lead to the home of the King who is holy, eternal and true-

For holy, you see-
is King Christ JESUS, the Almighty.

Come to My realm of deliverance-
as you bow in the midst of My holy presence.

For holy and true-
is the King who truly loves you.

Trust and Hope in *The King of Kings*

Christ *Jesus,* the Forever-Living King Speaking

Dear Children-
O Blessed Nation.

Put Your *Full Trust In Your Mighty King-*
As You *Join My Heavenly Choir As They Sing.*

For *Holy And True-*
Are My Heavenly Choirs That *Sing With Blessed You.*

Lift Up Your Voice And *Give Me Praise-*
As I Walk With You *During These Pandemic Days.*

For *Holy And True-*
Is The King Who Gracefully Sees You Through.

WHEN THE KING CALLS YOU

CHRIST JESUS, THE FOREVER-LIVING KING SPEAKING

WHEN *THE HOLY KING OF THE HEAVENS CALL*-
I WILL HOLD ON TO MY LOVED ONES, SO THAT *THEY WILL NOT FALL.*

FOR THE GATES THAT *LEAD TO EVERLASTING DESTRUCTION*- HAVE OPENED WIDE, SO THAT THEY MAY *CAPTURE AND SWALLOW MY VULNERABLE AND WEAK CHILDREN.*

MY CHILDREN-
O BLESSED SOULS FROM EVERY NATION-

CAPTURE MY HOLY CALL-
SO THAT *YOUR SOULS WILL NOT FALL.*

FOR *HOLY AND TRUE-*
IS THE GREAT KING OF PEACE, *WHO HAS CALLED YOU.*

COME, AND REJOICE WITH *CHRIST, THE FOREVER-LIVING KING*

CHRIST JESUS, THE FOREVER-LIVING KING SPEAKING

MY REJOICING GATES HAVE OPENED-
FOR *MY FAITHFUL CHILDREN.*

FOR *THEY HAVE FOLLOWED ME-*
INTO THE REALM OF SWEET ETERNITY.

THEY HAVE *ENTERED THE HOME, YOU SEE-*
OF THE *FOREVER REIGNING KING AND GOD ALMIGHTY.*

THEY HAVE *EARNED THE RIGHT-*
TO VISUALLY *PLACE ME WITHIN THEIR BLESSED SIGHT.*

FOR *THEY DO BELIEVE-*
IN THE HEAVEN SENT MESSAGES THAT *THEY DID RECEIVE.*

HOLY AND TRUE-
ARE THEY WHO *BELIEVE IN THE GREAT AND MIGHTY KING WHO HAS SEEN THEM THROUGH.*

HOLY, HOLY, HOLY-
IS THE ONE AND ONLY CHRIST ALMIGHTY!!!

WHEN YOU ARE *IN NEED OF THE KING*

CHRIST *JESUS,* THE FOREVER-LIVING KING SPEAKING

O BLESSED LOVED ONES OF MINE-
I AM AT YOUR BECKON CALL *DURING THIS CRITICAL PERIOD OF TIME.*

I CAN SEE-
EVERYTHING THAT HAS *AFFECTED THE VULNERABLE CHILDREN OF GOD ALMIGHTY.*

I CAN SEE-
THE NEEDS THAT HAVE *FOLLOWED THE CHILDREN WHO BELONG TO ME.*

FOR ON *MY THRONE OF LOVE-*
SIT THE GREATEST KING ALIVE, *ON EARTH, AND SWEET HEAVEN ABOVE.*

FOR *HOLY AND TRUE-*
IS THE KING WHO SPEAKS TO YOU.

I CAN HEAR YOUR WHISPERS, *O GREAT AND HOLY KING AND GOD*

<u>BARBARA SPEAKING OF KING JESUS</u>

HE WHISPERS TO ME *THROUGHOUT THE DAY-*
AND HE TELLS ME JUST WHAT *I SHOULD SAY.*

FOR *HE HAS SENT ME-*
TO REVEAL *THE TRUTH ABOUT GOD ALMIGHTY.*

I CAN HEAR HIM AS *HE WHISPERS TO ME THROUGHOUT THE NIGHT.*
I CAN SEE HIS HOLY SPIRIT, FOR *HE IS ALWAYS WITHIN MY SPIRITUAL SIGHT.*

I CAN HEAR *KING JESUS SPEAKING IN A VERY LOW VOICE.*
AS HE SPEAKS TO MY OBEDIENT SPIRIT, *MY MIND, BODY AND SOUL REJOICE.*

FOR *HOLY AND REAL-*
IS THE SPIRIT OF CHRIST, THE KING, THAT *MY ENTIRE BEING CAN TRULY SEE AND FEEL.*

HOLY, HOLY, HOLY-
ARE THE WHISPERS OF CHRIST JESUS, THE ALMIGHTY!!!

I WILL SEEK CHRIST, THE FOREVER-LIVING KING'S, FAITHFUL SUBJECTS TODAY

<u>BARBARA SPEAKING</u>

CHRIST JESUS, THE FOREVER-LIVING KING AND GOD, HAS SENT ME-
TO BRING TO HIM *THOSE WHO BELONG TO GOD ALMIGHTY.*

HE HAS SENT ME *TO RETRIEVE-*
THOSE WHO *DID RECEIVE.*

FOR *I AM SEEKING-*
THOSE WHO HAVE BEEN *OBEDIENT TO THE GREAT AND HOLY KING.*

CHRIST, THE KING, *HAS SENT ME, YOU SEE-*
TO LEAD BACK TO HIM *THOSE WHO WERE CHOSEN BY ALMIGHTY HE.*

FOR *HOLY AND TRUE-*
IS *THE KING WHO SENDS ME TO YOU.*

HE HAS FOUND, YOU SEE-
THE LOYAL SUBJECTS WHO *DWELL IN THE KINGDOM OF GOD ALMIGHTY.*

MY CHOSEN ONES WILL SEEK ME, AND I WILL FIND THEM, *SAYS CHRIST JESUS, THE FOREVER LIVING KING*

CHRIST JESUS, THE FOREVER-LIVING KING, SPEAKING

SEEK ME, MY LOVED ONES.
SEEK YOUR GREAT AND HOLY KING OF KINGS, *O BLESSED AND CHOSEN DAUGHTERS AND SONS.*

FOR, *I HAVE PERMITTED, YOU SEE-*
MY CHOSEN ONES TO FIND ME.

FOR, THROUGHOUT YOUR YEARS *YOU HAVE DONE YOUR THING-*
AND NOW, YOU HAVE BEEN CAPTURED BY THE ETERNAL ONE; CHRIST JESUS, YOUR HEAVENLY KING.

COME TO ME-
FOR YOU HAVE REACHED THE POINT OF TIME THAT *YOU WILL FOREVER FOLLOW CHRIST JESUS, THE ALMIGHTY.*

FOR *GOD, OUR HEAVENLY FATHER, YOU SEE-*
HAS *LED HIS CHOSEN LOVED ONES TO ME.*

FOR *HOLY AND TRUE-*
IS THE FATHER WHO HAS *SENT ME TO BLESSED AND BELOVED YOU.*

HOLY, HOLY, HOLY-
IS THE FATHER; JEHOVAH ALMIGHTY!!!

THE KING IS IN OUR MIDST TODAY

CHRIST JESUS, THE FOREVER-LIVING KING, SPEAKING

CAN YOU SEE? *CAN YOU SEE?*
CAN YOUR BLESSED SPIRIT *SEE MY VISIBILITY?*

FOR *MY WORKS ARE IN YOUR MIDST TODAY*-

OPEN YOUR EYES, DEAR ONES, *AND HEAR WHAT MY HOLY SPIRIT HAS TO SAY.*

FOR *I DO SPEAK TODAY, YOU SEE*-
THROUGH *THE MESSENGERS WHO ARE SENT BY ME.*

AND, *I HAVE SENT BARBARA:*
THEREFORE, DEAR ONES, *YOU MUST LISTEN TO MY CHOSEN DAUGHTER.*

FOR *SHE REVEALS THE TRUTH, YOU SEE*-
SHE REVEALS *THE TRUTH THAT COMES FROM ME.*

BELIEVE ME, DEAR ONES-
THAT I SEND BARBARA TO *MY SPIRITUALLY NEEDY AND CALLED DAUGHTERS AND SONS.*

FOR I, YOUR GREAT AND HOLY KING, *AM IN YOUR MIDST TODAY.*
COME, DEAR CHILDREN, AND *FOLLOW MY HOLY WAY!!!*

THE KING IS IN OUR MIDST

BARBARA SPEAKING

CHRIST, OUR VICTORIOUS GOD AND KING, *REJOICES IN OUR MIDST TODAY.*
FOR HE IS PLEASED WITH *THOSE WHO FOLLOW HIS LIFE REWARDING HOLY WAY.*

HE REJOICES IN THE PRESENCE OF *THE SPIRITUALLY WEAK ONES-*
AS HE REVEALS HIS HOLY WORDS TO *HIS NEEDY DAUGHTERS AND SONS.*

I WILL REJOICE TOO-
FOR I AM GLAD TO WITNESS THE JOY OF THOSE WHO ARE *FAITHFUL AND TRUE.*

FOR *CHRIST JESUS, OUR FOREVER REJOICING KING-*
HAS COME BACK TO US WITH *A POWERFUL HEAVENLY THING.*

HE HAS COME BACK TO US WITH *GREAT HEAVENLY MIGHT-*
AS HE KEEPS HIS EARTHLY CHILDREN *WITHIN HIS VICTORIOUS SIGHT.*

HOLY, HOLY, HOLY-
IS OUR GREAT LORD AND GOD ALMIGHTY!!!

CHRIST *JESUS,* THE FOREVER-LIVING KING, *HAS COME BACK TO EXPOSE SATAN*

CHRIST *JESUS,* THE FOREVER-LIVING KING, SPEAKING

I, YOUR LORD, GOD AND *KING JESUS, HAVE COME BACK TO EXPOSE HE-*
I HAVE COME BACK TO *EXPOSE HE WHO IS OUR EVERLASTING ENEMY.*

FOR *ONLY I, YOU SEE-*
HAVE THE DIVINE POWER TO *TERMINATE SATAN, OUR ENEMY.*

FOR *HE COMES TO DESTROY-*
EVERY *UNCLEAN GIRL AND BOY.*

BUT *I, THE GREAT AND HOLY KING, YOU SEE-*
WILL PURIFY THE *UNCLEAN ONES WHO TURN TO ME.*

FOR *HOLY AND TRUE-*
IS THE KING AND GOD WHO WILL *PURIFY BELOVED YOU.*

HOLY, HOLY, HOLY-
IS THE PURIFIER CALLED CHRIST ALMIGHTY!!

CHRIST, THE FOREVER-LIVING KING, *HAS RETURNED TO DESTROY THE WORKS OF SATAN*

CHRIST *JESUS,* THE FOREVER-LIVING KING, SPEAKING

I HAVE RETURNED, YOU SEE-
I HAVE COME BACK *TO DESTROY SATAN, MY ENEMY.*

FOR *HE TORTURES, YOU SEE-*
THE LOVED ONES OF *CHRIST ALMIGHTY.*

FOR I, THE LORD, KING AND GOD, *DOES HAVE THE DIVINE POWER-*
TO BATTLE SATAN'S REALM OF EVIL AND DESTRUCTION; *EVERY SECOND, MINUTE AND HOUR.*

FOR *I, THE VICTORIOUS ONE-*
WILL BATTLE THE GATES OF HELL FOR *MY WORTHY DAUGHTER AND SON.*

FOR *HOLY, ETERNAL AND TRUE-*
IS THE MIGHTY GOD AND KING WHO *FIGHTS FOR WELL-LOVED ME AND YOU.*

HOLY, HOLY, HOLY-
IS THE FOREVER RULING CHRIST ALMIGHTY!!!

CHRIST, THE HOLY KING, HAS RETURNED TO RECEIVE THE HALLELUJAHS

CHRIST JESUS, THE FOREVER-LIVING KING, SPEAKING

I, THE VICTORIOUS LORD, KING AND GOD, *HAVE RETURNED TO HEAR YOUR PRAISE.*
FOR I AM IN YOUR BLESSED MIDST, *DURING THESE PANDEMIC DAYS.*

AND *I DESIRE TO HEAR YOUR* HALLELUJAH-
FOR I HAVE BEEN *SENT BY OUR HOLY GOD AND FATHER,* JEHOVAH.

HE HAS SENT ME-
TO REVEAL HIS TRUTH AND MY DIVINITY.

FOR HOLY AND TRUE-
IS THE HEAVENLY GOD AND FATHER WHO HAS SENT BARBARA AND ME TO YOU.

HOLY, HOLY, HOLY-
IS OUR GOD AND FATHER, JEHOVAH ALMIGHTY!!!

FOR HE REIGNS, YOU SEE-
IN THE PRESENCE OF YOU AND ME.

HALLELUJAH! HALLELUJAH! HALLELUJAH-
TO OUR GOD AND FATHER JEHOVAH!!!

LET THE REALM OF PRAISE BOW IN THE PRESENCE OF CHRIST JESUS, THE HOLY ETERNAL KING

BARBARA SPEAKING

PRAISE! PRAISE! PRAISE!!!
LET THE SOUND OF PRAISE FLOW FROM OUR SPIRITS AND LIPS DURING THESE PANDEMIC DAYS!

LET THE HOLY KING HEAR-
THE SOUND OF PRAISE AS HE DRAWS NEAR.

FOR OUR PRAISE, YOU SEE-
WELCOMES THE GREAT HEAVENLY KING; CHRIST ALMIGHTY.

LET THE GATES OF DIVINE LAUGHTER-
WELCOME OUR KING, GOD, AND HEAVENLY FATHER.

For *King Jesus, you see-*
Is *the God and Father who created you and me.*

Praise Him! Praise Him! Praise Him today-
Let the sound of praise *lead us to the King's life saving holy way!*

For *His grace and joy-*
Have come to *rescue earth's needy little girl and boy.*

The *King has come, you see-*
To give *everlasting life to you and me.*

For *Holy, eternal and true-*
Is the mighty King who can *save me and you.*

Let the sound of *divine laughter and praise-*
Welcome *King Jesus throughout these life seeking days.*

For *Holy and true-*
Is the King and God who is *in the midst of me and you.*

Holy, holy, holy-
Is the King; Christ almighty!!!

Bowing in the holy presence of *the forever-ruling and living King of Kings*

<u>Barbara speaking</u>

I now bow, you see-
In the holy presence of *the mighty King who has rescued my family and me.*

MY *WEAK KNEES BEND, YOU SEE-*
IN THE HOLY PRESENCE OF *THE KING WHO HAS CHOSEN BLESSED ME.*

FOR *HE HAS CHOSEN ME-*
ALONG WITH THE LOVED ONES WHO *SIT AROUND THE THRONE OF GOD ALMIGHTY.*

I AM TRULY BLESSED-
THAT I HAVE BEEN *CHOSEN TO SIT AMONG GOD'S BEST.*

FOR *HOLY AND TRUE-*
ARE THEY WHO HAVE BEEN *CHOSEN BY THE HOLY KING WHO SEES HIS LOVED ONES THROUGH.*

THE HEAVENLY GATES HAVE OPENED FOR US, *AND WE WILL ENTER*

BARBARA SPEAKING

THE KING'S HEAVENLY GATES *HAVE OPENED WIDE FOR US.*
THEY HAVE OPENED IN *THE HOLY PRESENCE OF KING JESUS.*

WE WILL, WITH BOLDNESS, *WALK THROUGH-*
THE HEAVENLY GATES THAT *LEAD TO THE KING WHO IS ETERNAL AND TRUE.*

WE WILL ENTER-
THE HOLY GATES THAT *LEAD TO GOD, OUR HEAVENLY FATHER.*

FOR *HE APPROVES, YOU SEE-*
OF THE LOVE THAT *WE HAVE FOR THE KING ALMIGHTY.*

WE WILL ENTER-
YES! EVERY *CHOSEN MOTHER, FATHER, SON AND DAUGHTER.*

FOR *THE HEAVENLY GATES OF CHRIST JESUS-*
WELCOME BLESSED AND CHOSEN US.

AND HE SHALL REIGN *FOREVER AND EVER*

<u>BARBARA SPEAKING</u>

BEHOLD! BEHOLD! BEHOLD!
BEHOLD THE HEAVEN SENT THRONE AND KING THAT ARE *MORE VALUABLE THAN EARTH'S GATHERED GOLD.*

BEHOLD THE HEAVEN SENT KING WHO *SITS ON HIS MIGHTY THRONE.*
BEHOLD THE REIGNING KING *JESUS, FOR HE NEVER LEAVES US ALONE!*

BEHOLD HIS MAJESTY!
BEHOLD HIS HEAVENLY GLORY!

BEHOLD THE MIGHTY HOLY ONE!
BEHOLD GOD, THE FATHER'S, ONLY BEGOTTEN SON!!!

FOR *HE REIGNS IN OUR BLESSED MIDST.*
HE IS *THE ETERNAL KING WHO WILL FOREVER EXIST!!!*

IN THE MIDST OF *THE KING'S HEAVENLY GLORY*

<u>BARBARA SPEAKING</u>

I AM IN *THE HOLY KING'S MIDST-*
FOR I TRULY BELIEVE THAT *HE DOES EXIST.*

For *I have been permitted to witness-*
a taste of *His presence and holiness.*

I have seen, you see-
the visible works of *our King and God; Christ Almighty.*

I have seen His glory-
as He revealed to me, *the depth and meaning of His holy story.*

For *He has shared with me-*
the reality of *His heavenly beauty and glory.*

For *Holy and true-*
is the King Who *sits and walks in the midst of me and you.*

Give the victorious KING and God *continuous praise*

<u>Barbara Speaking</u>

My hands-
are lifted up to sweet heaven, as *I give praise to King Jesus, in the presence of His children who have come from many lands.*

United with *my sisters and brothers from many lands-*
in divine unity and love, *we lift up our praising hands.*

For we give *continuous praise, you see-*
for *our victorious Christ Almighty.*

For *holy, eternal and true-*
is the heavenly king who *rules and reigns over me and you.*

Holy, holy, holy-
is our everlasting king; Christ almighty!!!

For *he reigns in our midst-*
and we give him continuous praise, *for he truly exist.*

Holy, holy, holy-
is existing Christ almighty!!!

And his mighty throne *is in our midst today*

<u>**Barbara speaking**</u>

He sits on his mighty throne *in our blessed midst today-*
come, dear brothers and sisters, and let us listen to what the king has to say.

<u>**Barbara speaking to Christ, the KING**</u>

I can feel your holy presence *King JESUS-*
as you sit on your holy throne *in the midst of us.*

Although you and your mighty throne *are not visible to many-*
I can see your visibility, as you sit on your throne in the presence of God, our heavenly father, *who is also known as sweet eternity.*

FOR, *IN OUR MIDST, YOU SEE-*
I CAN FEEL *YOUR HOLY PRESENCE AND YOUR VISIBILITY.*

FOR *YOUR HOLY SPIRIT, YOU SEE-*
HAS GRANTED ME THE PRIVILEGE AND HONOR TO *SEE MY GREAT AND HOLY KING; CHRIST ALMIGHTY.*

HOLY, HOLY, HOLY-
IS THE VISIBILITY OF GOD ALMIGHTY!!!

THE HOLY SCEPTER OF *CHRIST, THE* KING

<u>BARBARA SPEAKING TO KING JESUS</u>

O HOLY KING AND GOD-
O GREAT ONE, WHO BRINGS TO EARTH'S LANDS, *YOUR VERSION OF HEAVENLY LOVE.*

I CAN SEE *YOUR DIVINE SCEPTER.*
FOR YOU HAVE MADE IT VISIBLE TO ME, *YOUR FAITHFUL AND OBEDIENT DAUGHTER.*

THE SCEPTER OF THE HOLY KING OF KINGS-
REVEALS TO ME *HEAVENLY THINGS.*

THE SCEPTER OF CHRIST JESUS-
DELIVERS A MESSAGE THAT WILL *SAVE US.*

FOR *KING* JESUS, *YOU SEE-*
HOLY SCEPTER IS IN THE MIDST OF *THE CHILDREN WHO ARE CALLED AND CHOSEN BY GOD ALMIGHTY.*

HOLY, HOLY, HOLY-
IS THE SCEPTER OF CHRIST ALMIGHTY!!!

DO NOT SEARCH FOR CHRIST JESUS, THE FOREVER-LIVING KING

BARBARA SPEAKING

DO NOT SEARCH, YOU SEE-
FOR *THE HEAVENLY KING CALLED CHRIST ALMIGHTY.*

FOR *HE DOES SEEK-*
THE *STRONG AND THE MEEK.*

HE IS *THE ONLY ONE-*
WHO SEEKS AND FINDS *HIS WANDERING DAUGHTER AND SON.*

YOU CANNOT, YOU SEE-
SEEK AND FIND, *THE HEAVENLY KING; CHRIST ALMIGHTY.*

FOR *HIS HOLY PLAN-*
IS TO ASSIST AND DELIVER *HIS CHOSEN WOMAN, CHILD, AND MAN.*

THEREFORE, *YOU CANNOT FIND, YOU SEE-*
THE KING AND GOD WHO *SEEKS THE LOVED ONES OF GOD ALMIGHTY.*

YOU CANNOT FIND-
A LOVE AND, *THE GOD WHO IS ONE OF A KIND.*

THEREFORE, *MY SISTER AND BROTHER-*
YOU MUST *PRAY CONTINUOUSLY TO GOD, THE FATHER.*

FOR *ONLY HE-*
CAN FIND THE LOVED ONES WHO ARE *CHOSEN BY GOD ALMIGHTY.*

PRAY! PRAY! PRAY!
PRAY THAT *KING JESUS HAS CHOSEN YOU TO WALK TOWARDS HIS LIFE SAVING HOLY WAY.*

HOLY, HOLY, HOLY-
IS THE WAY THAT *LEADS TO THE LIFE SAVING KING AND GOD ALMIGHTY!!!*

SEEK, SEEK, SEEK

CHRIST JESUS, THE FOREVER-LIVING KING, SPEAKING

I SOUGHT MY CHOSEN ONES-
AND I HAVE FOUND MY WORTHY DAUGHTERS AND SONS.

FOR IN THE BEGINNING-
THEY WERE CHOSEN FOR CHRIST, THE EVER-LASTING KING.

THEY WERE CHOSEN, YOU SEE-
BY JEHOVAH, GOD ALMIGHTY.

THEY WERE BLESSED FROM THE BEGINNING OF TIME;
AND NOW, THEY ARE MINE.

COME, MY LOVELY ONES!
COME AND SIT WITH ME AT MY HEAVENLY THRONE.

FOR YOU HAVE BEEN FAITHFUL, YOU SEE-
TO YOUR SAVING KING, THE FOREVER-LIVING CHRIST ALMIGHTY.

COME! COME! COME!
AND ENTER MY GLORIOUS HEAVENLY KINGDOM!!!

SEEK, AND YOU WILL FIND, THE HOLY KING WHO HAS CHOSEN YOU

CHRIST *JESUS,* THE FOREVER-LIVING *KING,* SPEAKING

DEAR LOVED ONE-
DO NOT FLEE FROM *GOD, THE FATHER'S, ONLY BEGOTTEN SON.*

SEEK THE HEAVEN SENT KING-
WHO HAS CHOSEN YOU TO BE *INCLUDED IN HIS GLORIOUS AND WONDERFUL THING.*

DO NOT FLEE-
FROM *THE HOLY CALL OF GOD ALMIGHTY.*

FOR *I HAVE CHOSEN-*
YOU TO BE *ONE OF MY BLESSED CHILDREN.*

DO NOT RUN FROM ME-
DO NOT RUN FROM *CHRIST, THE KING ALMIGHTY.*

FOR *YOU WERE CHOSEN, YOU SEE-*
BY THE DIVINE POWER AND LOVE OF *THE FOREVER-REIGNING CHRIST ALMIGHTY.*

SIT STILL-
AND FOLLOW MY HOLY WILL.

FOR *YOU HAVE BEEN CHOSEN, YOU SEE-*
BY THE HEAVEN SENT GOD ALMIGHTY.

HOLY, HOLY, HOLY-
ARE THE CHOSEN SONS AND DAUGHTERS OF GOD ALMIGHTY!!!

THE MIGHTY *THRONE OF THE DIVINE KING*

BARBARA SPEAKING

THE MIGHTY THRONE OF KING JESUS-
HAS DESCENDED, AND IS IN THE MIDST OF US.

FOR HIS MIGHTY THRONE OF LOVE-
HAS VISITED US FROM SWEET HEAVEN ABOVE.

UPON THE KING'S THRONE OF LOVE-
SITS THE HOLY ONE FROM HEAVEN ABOVE.

FOR KING JESUS' MIGHTY THRONE, YOU SEE-
NOW SITS IN THE MIDST OF YOU AND ME.

HOLY, HOLY, HOLY-
IS THE THRONE OF CHRIST, THE ALMIGHTY!!!

HE, CHRIST, THE KING, LED ME TO HIS MIGHTY THRONE OF LOVE

BARBARA SPEAKING

I DID NOT SEEK-
THE KING WHO RULES AND REIGNS OVER THE STRONG AND THE MEEK.

FOR KING JESUS, YOU SEE-
LED WANDERING ME.

HE LED ME, YOU SEE-
TO THE MIGHTY THRONE OF GOD ALMIGHTY.

FOR, I AM, YOU SEE-
ONE OF THE CHOSEN WHO BELONGS TO CHRIST ALMIGHTY.

HE LED ME *THROUGH THE YEARS-*
HE LED AND GUIDED ME *IN THE MIDST OF MY FEARS.*

HE LED ME *TO HIS MIGHTY THRONE-*
AND HE TOLD ME THAT *I AM NEVER ALONE.*

HE LED ME *THROUGHOUT THE DAY-*
HE HELD MY HAND, AND *HE LED ME TO HIS LIFE REWARDING HOLY WAY.*

OH HOW GRATEFUL-
TO BE ONE OF THE CHOSEN OF *THE GOD AND KING WHO IS GRAND AND WONDERFUL.*

THE HOLY WORKS OF *THE KING AND I*

BARBARA SPEAKING

DEAR BROTHERS AND SISTERS OF MINE-
I AM LEADING YOU TO CHRIST, OUR EVERLASTING KING, *DURING THIS PANDEMIC PERIOD OF TIME.*

FOR *THE WORKS THAT WE DO-*
WILL DRAW YOU TO *THE HEAVENLY KING WHO IS HOLY, ETERNAL AND TRUE.*

WITNESS! WITNESS! WITNESS!
WITNESS KING JESUS' PRESENCE AND HOLINESS.

FOR, *THROUGH PURIFIED ME-*
YOU WILL *WITNESS THE WORKS OF GOD ALMIGHTY.*

HIS WORKS ARE GOOD, YOU SEE-
FOR *HE WORKS THROUGH BLESSED SENT ME.*

HE FEEDS THE HUNGRY-
WITH THE HEAVENLY NOURISHMENT THAT *COMES FROM GOD ALMIGHTY.*

HIS HOLY WORDS, YOU SEE-
IS THE FOOD THAT *COMES FROM THE HEAVENLY KING, CHRIST ALMIGHTY.*

I WILL DELIVER TO EVERY CHILD, WOMAN AND MAN-
THE FOOD THAT *COMES FROM THE KING'S MIGHTY HAND.*

FOR *HOLY AND TRUE-*
IS THE NOURISHMENT THAT *GOD SENDS TO ME AND YOU.*

HOLY, HOLY, HOLY-
IS THE FOOD THAT *DESCENDS FROM THE HAND OF GOD ALMIGHTY!!!*

CHRIST, THE KING, *IS MY EVERYTHING*

BARBARA SPEAKING

HE IS MY EVERYTHING-
HE IS MY GOD, AND *HE IS EVERLASTING.*

HE IS *CHRIST JESUS, GOD, THE FATHER'S, ONLY BEGOTTEN SON.*
HE IS *THE FOREVER EXISTING ONE.*

HE IS CHRIST JESUS-
HE IS THE HEAVEN SENT KING WHO *WALKS IN THE MIDST OF US.*

FOR, *THROUGH ME-*
CHRIST *JESUS, THE HOLY KING, REVEALS HIS VISIBILITY.*

FOR *HOLY AND REAL-*
IS THE PRESENCE OF THE KING THAT *THE TRUSTING ONES CAN TRULY FEEL.*

HOLY, HOLY, HOLY-
IS THE VISIBILITY OF CHRIST ALMIGHTY!!!

HE IS MY EVERYTHING-
HE IS THE HOLY KING!!!

DEAR BROTHERS AND SISTERS: *LET US MAKE CHRIST, THE KING, OUR EVERYTHING*

<u>BARBARA SPEAKING</u>

DEAR SISTER AND BROTHER-
IN HONOR OF *KING JESUS, OUR ORIGIN, CREATOR AND FATHER-*

LET US *COME TOGETHER AS ONE-*
AND GIVE HOMAGE TO *KING JESUS, FOR HE IS GOD, THE FATHER'S, ONLY BEGOTTEN SON.*

LET US MAKE *CHRIST, THE FOREVER REIGNING KING-*
OUR EVERYTHING.

FOR *HE IS HOLY AND TRUE-*
AND *HE DOES RULE OVER BELIEVING ME AND YOU.*

LET US BOW AS ONE, *IN THE HOLY PRESENCE OF OUR HEAVEN SENT KING-*
AS YOU AND I *MAKE HIM OUR EVERYTHING.*

FOR *HOLY AND TRUE-*
IS THE KING WHO REALLY LOVES ME AND YOU.

HOLY, HOLY, HOLY-
IS OUR EVERYTHING; CHRIST ALMIGHTY!!!

HE REIGNS TODAY, YOU SEE-
IN THE MIDST OF *YOU AND ME.*

HOLY, HOLY, HOLY-
IS OUR EVERYTHING, CALLED CHRIST ALMIGHTY!!!

DO NOT REVERE SATAN! DO NOT REVERE SATAN! DO NOT REVERE SATAN, *SAYS THE HEAVEN SENT KING JESUS!!!*

CHRIST *JESUS*, THE FOREVER-LIVING *KING*, SPEAKING

MY CHILDREN-
DO NOT *REVERE SATAN!*

DO NOT GIVE HIM *THE RESPECT AND HONOR, YOU SEE-*
THAT *BELONGS ONLY TO ME!!!*

FOR *YOU DO NOT KNOW-*
THAT THE REVERENCE THAT YOU GIVE TO SATAN, *FOLLOWS YOU WHEREVER YOU GO.*

DO NOT ACKNOWLEDGE HIS "UNHOLY" WORKS AND DEEDS *IN MY HOLY PRESENCE.*
DO NOT INVITE HIM AND HIS DEMONS *INTO YOUR EARTHLY RESIDENCE.*

FOR THE RESPECT AND ACKNOWLEDGMENT THAT *YOU GIVE TO SATAN, MY ENEMY-*
BELONG SOLELY TO *YOUR GOD AND HOLY KING; CHRIST ALMIGHTY.*

DO NOT *FOLLOW HIS WICKED WAYS,*
AND EXPECT ME TO HELP YOU *DURING YOUR TROUBLED DAYS.*

FOR *SATAN, IN REALITY-*
IS TRULY *YOUR ENEMY.*

THEREFORE, DEAR ONES.
DO NOT GIVE HONOR AND RESPECT TO SATAN, IF YOU *TRULY DESIRE TO BE MY CHOSEN DAUGHTERS AND SONS.*

FOR *I WILL NOT, YOU SEE-*
SHARE YOUR WORLD WITH *SATAN, OUR ENEMY.*

THEREFORE, DEAR CHILDREN-
YES! *YOU FROM EVERY NATION.*

YOU MUST GIVE GLORY AND HONOR TO *THE FOREVER-LIVING GOD ALMIGHTY.*
DEAR CHILDREN: YOU MUST GIVE REVERENCE *ONLY TO ME!!!*

THERE ARE *NO EXCEPTION-*
IF YOU WANT TO BE *MY FAITHFUL CHILDREN.*

DEAR CHILDREN: *FLEE! FLEE! FLEE!*
FLEE FROM SATAN, OUR ENEMY!!!

DO NOT GIVE SATAN REVERENCE, *SAYS THE HEAVEN SENT KING JESUS!!!*

CHRIST *JESUS,* THE FOREVER-LIVING *KING,* SPEAKING

DO NOT GIVE SATAN *REVERENCE IN YOUR DANCE-*
FOR HE WILL *CAUSE YOUR DESTRUCTION IN JUST ONE GLANCE.*

DO NOT SLEEP WITH *SATAN, YOUR ENEMY-*
FOR YOU DO THIS, DEAR CHILDREN, WHEN YOU SLEEP WITH, OR HAVE SEXUAL RELATIONS WITH ONE WHO IS *NOT APPROVED BY HOLY ME.*

THEREFORE, *DEAR ONES-*
YOU MUST LIVE HOLY, FOR *YOU ARE MY LONGED FOR DAUGHTERS AND SONS.*

DO NOT USE BAD OR INAPPROPRIATE LANGUAGE *IN MY HOLY PRESENCE,*
FOR YOU WILL *NOT BE INVITED TO MY HEAVENLY RESIDENCE.*

WALK UPRIGHT *IN MY HOLY PRESENCE-*
FOR WITHIN ME, YOU WILL FIND *A PERMANENT HEAVENLY RESIDENCE.*

FLEE FROM *YOUR SINFUL WAYS-*
AND GIVE YOUR GREAT AND HOLY KING AND GOD, *CONTINUOUS PRAISE!!!*

KING *JESUS* SAVES US

CHRIST *JESUS,* THE FOREVER-LIVING *KING,* SPEAKING

I WILL SAVE, YOU SEE-
THE BLESSED ONES WHO *FOLLOW ME.*

FOR *I DESIRE, YOU SEE-*
THAT MY RIGHTEOUS ONES *FOLLOW HOLY ME.*

I WILL SAVE THOSE WHO *BELIEVE IN MY LIFE REWARDING POWER-*
THAT FLOWS IN THE MIDST OF THE RIGHTEOUS ONES, *EVERY SECOND, MINUTE AND HOUR.*

I WILL LEAD THEM TO *THE HOME, YOU SEE-*
OF THE *FOREVER-LIVING KING ALMIGHTY.*

FOR *HOLY AND TRUE-*
IS THE GLORIOUS KING WHO *SAVES RIGHTEOUS YOU.*

I AM IN YOUR BLESSED PRESENCE-
AND I WALK IN THE MIDST OF *YOUR EARTHLY RESIDENCE.*

FOR *HOLY AND REAL-*
IS THE HEAVENLY KING'S PRESENCE THAT *THE RIGHTEOUS ONES DO FEEL.*

HOLY, HOLY, HOLY-
IS THE PRESENCE OF GOD ALMIGHTY!!!

I HAVE COME TO SAVE THE RIGHTEOUS ONES, SAYS KING JESUS

CHRIST JESUS, THE FOREVER-LIVING KING, SPEAKING

O RIGHTEOUS CHILDREN OF MINE-
I AM WITH YOU DURING THIS PANDEMIC PERIOD OF TIME.

FOR I HAVE COME BACK, YOU SEE-
TO SAVE THE RIGHTEOUS CHILDREN WHO BELONG TO ME.

I HAVE COME, YOU SEE-
TO REWARD AND RETRIEVE THE HOLY.

FOR MY RIGHTEOUS ONES-
ARE TRULY MY HEAVEN BOUND DAUGHTERS AND SONS.

FOR HOLY AND TRUE-
IS THE KING WHO HAS COME FOR YOU.

HOLY, HOLY, HOLY-
IS THE RETRIEVING KING AND GOD; CHRIST ALMIGHTY!!!

REJOICE, DEAR EARTH, FOR CHRIST, THE FOREVER VICTORIOUS KING, HAS RETURNED!!!

CHRIST JESUS, THE FOREVER-LIVING KING, SPEAKING

REJOICE, DEAR ONES!
FOR KING JESUS HAS RETURNED TO SAVE HIS DAUGHTERS AND SONS!

REJOICE THROUGHOUT YOUR LANDS-
FOR YOUR DESTINY *IS IN THE HEAVENLY KING'S LIFE SAVING HOLY HANDS!*

FOR *I AM IN THE MIDST, YOU SEE-*
OF THE WORLD THAT *DOESN'T BELIEVE IN ME.*

FOR *I HAVE RETURNED, YOU SEE-*
TO *PROVE AND REVEAL MY REALITY.*

FOR *I, YOUR LORD AND GOD DO EXIST-*
FOR *I, DEAR CHILDREN, AM IN YOUR MIDST.*

I MOVE AMONG YOU-
I AM *THE KING WHO HAS COME TO HELP YOU THROUGH.*

I WILL *HELP THOSE, YOU SEE-*
WHO *BELIEVE IN LIFE SAVING ME.*

THEREFORE, *REJOICE! REJOICE! REJOICE!*
LET HEAVEN AND EARTH *HEAR YOUR PRAISING VOICE!*

FOR, *I ALONE-*
CAN HEAR THE PRAISES THAT *REACH MY HEAVENLY THRONE.*

REJOICE! REJOICE! REJOICE!
LET YOUR HOLY KING *HEAR YOUR UNITED VOICE!*

FOR *I HAVE RETURNED, YOU SEE-*
TO HELP THE LOVED ONES WHO *BELONG TO ME!!!*

HOLY, HOLY, HOLY-
IS THE REJOICING KING ALMIGHTY!!!

THE KING HAS RETURNED *TO HELP HIS DECEIVED CHILDREN*

CHRIST JESUS, THE FOREVER-LIVING KING, SPEAKING

I HAVE RETURNED, YOU SEE-
TO HELP THOSE WHO WERE *DECEIVED BY SATAN, MY ENEMY.*

FOR *THROUGH BARBARA-*
I HAVE REVEALED SATAN'S "UNHOLY" PRESENCE *TO MY VULNERABLE SON AND DAUGHTER.*

FOR THEY HAVE BEEN *DECEIVED, YOU SEE-*
BY SATAN, THE "UNHOLY" ONE, *WHO HAS STOLEN THEM FROM ME.*

BUT I, *THE GREAT AND HOLY KING JESUS, YOU SEE-*
WILL *DEFEAT SATAN, MY ENEMY.*

FOR *HOLY, HOLY, HOLY-*
IS THE VICTORIOUS CHRIST ALMIGHTY!!!

AND CHRIST, THE FOREVER-LIVING KING AND GOD, *IS IN OUR BLESSED MIDST TODAY*

BARBARA SPEAKING

HE WALKS THE EARTH-
AS HE DID WHEN THE WORLD *CELEBRATED HIS FORETOLD HEAVEN SENT BIRTH.*

CHRIST, THE FOREVER-LIVING KING, MOVES IN OUR MIDST-
AS HIS MIRACLES *CONFIRM THAT HE DOES EXIST.*

HE IS REALLY *IN OUR MIDST, DEAR ONES-*
AND *HE SPEAKS TO HIS WORTHY DAUGHTER AND SON.*

FOR *THROUGH ME-*
KING *JESUS, REVEALS HIS VISIBILITY.*

HOLY, HOLY, HOLY-
IS THE *VISIBILITY OF CHRIST ALMIGHTY!!!*

REJOICE! REJOICE! REJOICE! *FOR YOU ARE IN THE PRESENCE OF OUR GOD AND FOREVER-REJOICING* KING

CHRIST *JESUS,* THE FOREVER-LIVING KING, SPEAKING

REJOICE, O BLESSED CHOSEN ONES!
FOR YOU ARE IN THE HOLY PRESENCE OF *THE KING WHO HAS COME FOR HIS BLESSED DAUGHTERS AND SONS.*

REJOICE WITH *GLADNESS IN YOUR HEARTS!*
REJOICE, DEAR CHILDREN, *BEFORE THE NEW DAY STARTS!*

FOR *CHRIST* JESUS, *YOUR ETERNAL KING-*
HAS COME BACK TO YOU *WITH A GLORIOUS THING.*

FOR THROUGH *BARBARA, MY SENT MESSENGER-*
I NOW SPEAK FACE TO FACE *TO MY STRAYING SON AND DAUGHTER.*

REJOICE IN THE MIDST OF YOUR LANDS-
FOR I, THE LORD GOD AND KING, HAVE PLACED YOU WITHIN MY POWERFUL SAVING HANDS.

REJOICE! REJOICE! REJOICE!
LET ME HEAR *YOUR TRUSTING VOICE!*

FOR *I, YOUR LORD AND GOD-*
DESIRE THAT YOU *EXPERIENCE A TASTE OF MY GLORY AND DIVINE LOVE.*

REJOICE, O BLESSED ONES!
REJOICE IN THE PRESENCE OF *THE MIGHTY KING WHO SAVES HIS WORTHY DAUGHTERS AND SONS!!!*

CHRIST, THE FOREVER-LIVING KING, *HAS RETURNED TO WEED OUT SATAN'S EVIL ANGELS*

<u>CHRIST JESUS, THE FOREVER-LIVING KING, SPEAKING</u>

I HAVE RETURNED, SO THAT *I MAY-*
MAKE KNOWN, THE EVIL ANGELS WHO HAVE CREPT IN THE MIDST OF MY UNSUSPECTING LOVED ONES ON EARTH TODAY.

I HAVE COME BACK, SO THAT *I MAY EXPOSE THE EVIL ONES AND SATAN, THEIR HELL BOUND FATHER.*
I HAVE RETURNED, SO THAT *I MAY REMOVE FROM SATAN'S EVIL CLUTCHES, MY CAPTURED SON AND DAUGHTER.*

FOR *SATAN, YOU SEE-*
IS THE REALM OF EVIL WHO HAS *TAKEN MANY WHO DID NOT BELIEVE IN ALMIGHTY ME.*

FOR *HOLY AND TRUE-*
IS THE KING WHO IS *VICTORIOUS OVER THE REALM OF EVIL THAT TORTURES AND DECEIVES ALL OF YOU.*

THE KING HAS RETURNED! THE KING HAS RETURNED! *THE KING HAS RETURNED!!!*

CHRIST *JESUS*, THE FOREVER-LIVING *KING*, SPEAKING

I HAVE RETURNED, *AND I AM IN YOUR MIDST!*
I HAVE COME BACK THROUGH *BARBARA, MY PURIFIED MESSENGER, SO THAT YOU MAY KNOW THAT I, CHRIST JESUS, DO EXIST.*

I, YOUR LORD, GOD AND KING, YOU SEE-
HAVE COME BACK, SO THAT YOU MAY HAVE AN OPPORTUNITY *TO WITNESS THE POWER THAT COMES FROM ME.*

FOR, THROUGH *BARBARA, MY MESSENGER AND BRIDE-*
I NOW, RELEASE A DIVINE LOVE FOR MY CHOSEN ONES THAT *I WILL NOT HIDE.*

FOR *SATAN, THE DEVIL, YOU SEE-*
HAS STOLEN *THE WEAK SOULS FROM ME.*

FOR THEY DID NOT REALLY *BELIEVE NOR FOLLOW, YOU SEE-*
THE HOLY KING CALLED *CHRIST ALMIGHTY.*

I HAVE RETURNED *IN THE MIDST OF EVERY LAND.*
I HAVE RETURNED *TO HELP EVERY CHOSEN WOMAN AND MAN.*

HOLY, HOLY, HOLY-
IS THE VISIBILITY OF CHRIST ALMIGHTY!!!

IF YOU WOULD FOLLOW MY HOLY WAY, *SAYS KING JESUS*

CHRIST *JESUS*, THE FOREVER-LIVING *KING*, SPEAKING

IF YOU WOULD FOLLOW ME, *SAYS CHRIST, THE KING-*
I WOULD LEAD YOU TO *A WONDERFUL AND EVERLASTING THING.*

I WOULD LEAD YOU TO *MY HEAVENLY HOME OF LOVE-*
WHERE MY LOVED ONES AND THRONE *SIT HIGH ABOVE.*

ABOVE THE BLUE SKY-
SITS *MY MIGHTY THRONE ON HIGH.*

ABOVE *THE BRIGHTEST STAR-*
DWELLS THE THRONE OF YOUR HEAVENLY KING, *WHICH ISN'T VERY FAR.*

IF YOU WOULD FOLLOW *THE WORKS OF MY HOLY HAND-*
MY HOLY SPIRIT WOULD *LEAD YOU TO MY PROMISED LAND.*

FOR *HOLY, YOU SEE-*
ARE THE BLESSED ONES WHO *FOLLOW THE GREAT AND HOLY KING ALMIGHTY.*

FOLLOW ME! FOLLOW ME!
FOLLOW *THE HOLY SPIRIT OF GOD ALMIGHTY!!!*

THE WORDS THAT FLOW FROM *THE MOUTH AND SOUL OF THE "UNREPENTANT" ONE*

<u>CHRIST JESUS, THE FOREVER-LIVING KING, SPEAKING</u>

THE WORDS THAT FLOW FROM *THE SOUL OF THE "UNREPENTANT" ONE-*
REVEAL THAT THEY ARE *SATAN'S DECEIVED DAUGHTER AND SON.*

FOR THOSE WHO *DO NOT REPENT, YOU SEE-*
CANNOT SHARE THE THRONE AND *DIVINE JOY THAT COME WITH FOLLOWING HOLY ME.*

FOR THE *"UNREPENTANT" SINNER*-
IS NOT *MY WORTHY SON OR DAUGHTER.*

FOR THEY ARE *THE "UNHOLY" ONES*-
THEY ARE TRULY *SATAN'S DECEIVED DAUGHTERS AND SONS.*

THE WORDS OF *THE HOLY KING*

BARBARA SPEAKING

I HAVE RECEIVED THE HOLY WORDS THAT WERE *REVEALED TO ME FROM CHRIST, THE KING OF KINGS-*
AND I WILL SHARE WITH MY EARTHLY BROTHERS AND SISTERS *THE WONDERFUL HEAVEN SENT THINGS.*

FOR *KING JESUS, YOU SEE-*
HAS *REVEALED HEAVENLY THINGS TO ME.*

FOR THE HEAVEN SENT WORDS THAT *DESCENDED FROM KING JESUS-*
WILL *HELP AND GUIDE ALL OF US.*

FOR *THE KING'S HOLY WORDS, YOUR SEE-*
WILL *BENEFIT BLESSED YOU AND ME.*

FOR *HOLY AND TRUE-*
ARE THE HEAVENLY WORDS THAT *KING JESUS HAS GIVEN TO ME AND YOU.*

HIS HOLY WORDS *LEAD TO HIS BOOK OF LIFE-*
WHICH INCLUDES THE NAMES OF *THE CHOSEN AND BLESSED HUSBAND AND WIFE.*

FOR *HOLY AND REWARDING, YOU SEE-*

ARE THE WORDS THAT COME FROM *THE SPIRIT OF GOD ALMIGHTY.*

HOLY, HOLY, HOLY-
ARE THE VALUABLE WORDS OF CHRIST ALMIGHTY!!!

WHEN CHRIST, THE FOREVER-LIVING KING, SOUNDS HIS GLORIOUS BELLS

<u>BARBARA SPEAKING</u>

WHEN CHRIST JESUS, *THE MIGHTY KING OF KINGS, SOUNDS HIS GLORIOUS BELLS IN MY MIDST-*
I PROCLAIM THE GOODNESS OF THE KING, *AS MY BLESSED PRESENCE AND LIPS CONFIRM THAT HE DOES EXIST.*

WHEN HIS HOLY BELLS *RING WITHIN MY EARTHLY RESIDENCE-*
I GO OUT TO HIS CALLED AND CHOSEN LOVED ONES *AND SHARE HIS HOLY PRESENCE.*

FOR HIS HOLY SPIRIT *AND PRESENCE, YOU SEE-*
DWELL WITHIN PURIFIED ME.

<u>BARBARA SPEAKING TO KING JESUS</u>

I CAN HEAR *YOUR GLORIOUS BELLS, O BLESSED KING;*
AND I WILL RECEIVE *YOUR HOLY WORDS AS YOUR BELLS RING.*

FOR *THE SOUND OF YOUR HOLY BELLS, YOU SEE-*
RELEASES *THE HOLY WORDS THAT YOU GIVE TO ME.*

FOR *HOLY AND REAL-*
ARE THE KING'S GLORIOUS BELLS THAT *I CAN TRULY HEAR AND FEEL.*

FOR *YOUR HOLY WORDS THAT I RECEIVE-*
HELP THOSE WHO ARE *STRUGGLING TO BELIEVE.*

HOLY, HOLY, HOLY-
ARE THE BELLS (WORDS) OF CHRIST ALMIGHTY!!!

I WILL SIT AND LISTEN TO THE KING, *AS HE SPEAKS HIS HOLY WORDS TO ME*

<u>BARBARA SPEAKING</u>

I AM SEATED, YOU SEE-
IN THE HOLY PRESENCE OF *CHRIST* JESUS; *THE ALMIGHTY.*

I WILL PAY ATTENTION-
FOR HE REVEALS TO ME VERY IMPORTANT THINGS THAT *HE WANTS ME TO SHARE WITH HIS CALLED AND CHOSEN CHILDREN.*

I WILL SIT VERY STILL-
FOR I WANT TO UNDERSTAND *HIS HOLY WORDS AND WILL.*

I WILL REMAIN SEATED IN HIS HOLY PRESENCE-
AS I RECEIVE HIS HOLY WORDS *IN THE MIDST OF MY RESIDENCE.*

I WILL LISTEN-
AS THE KING TELLS ME THE NEWS THAT *HE COMMANDS ME TO SHARE WITH HIS EARTHLY CHILDREN.*

I WILL NOT MOVE, YOU SEE-
UNTIL THE KING HAS *FINISHED SPEAKING TO ME.*

FOR *HOLY AND TRUE-*
ARE THE WORDS THAT ARE GIVEN TO ME AND YOU.

I WILL SIT VERY QUIETLY-

AS I WRITE DOWN *THE HOLY WORDS THAT ARE GIVEN TO ME FROM CHRIST ALMIGHTY.*

CHRIST, THE FOREVER-LIVING KING, *WHISPERS*

<u>CHRIST, THE FOREVER-LIVING KING, SPEAKING TO BARBARA</u>

MY DEAR BARBARA-
LISTEN VERY CLOSELY, FOR I AM WHISPERING MY WORDS OF SALVATION TO YOU, *MY SENT MESSENGER AND OBEDIENT DAUGHTER.*

I AM WHISPERING TO YOU TODAY-
SO THAT YOU MAY REVEAL TO MY LOVED ONES, *THE SECRET THAT WILL LEAD THEM TO MY LIFE SAVING AND REWARDING HOLY WAY.*

TELL THEM FOR ME, *DEAR BARBARA-*
TELL MY CALLED AND *CHOSEN SON AND DAUGHTER.*

TELL THEM TODAY-
THE IMPORTANCE OF *FOLLOWING MY ONLY WAY.*

FOR THERE IS *NO OTHER WAY, YOU SEE-*
THAT LEADS TO *THE EVERLASTING KINGDOM OF CHRIST ALMIGHTY.*

TELL THEM FOR ME, DEAR ONE-
THAT *I AM SEEKING MY CONFUSED DAUGHTER AND SON.*

I MOVE WHEN CHRIST JESUS, THE KING OF KINGS, SUMMONS ME

BARBARA SPEAKING TO HER BLESSED BEING

MOVE, O BLESSED SPIRIT!
SPEAK KING JESUS' HOLY WORDS, SO THAT THE CALLED ONES MAY HEAR IT!

MOVE, O BLESSED FEET THAT BELONG TO BARBARA!
DELIVER THE KING'S HOLY WORDS TO HIS STARVING SON AND DAUGHTER.

MOVE FAST-
SO THAT THEIR SPIRITUAL HUNGER WILL BE THAT OF THE PAST!

MOVE, O BLESSED SOUL, IN THE PRESENCE OF KING JESUS!
MOVE, O BLESSED SOUL, AS YOU RECEIVE THE HOLY WORDS THAT WILL SAVE US!

FOR CHRIST, THE FOREVER-LIVING KING, YOU SEE-
HAS COMMISSIONED TRUST WORTHY ME.

MOVE! MOVE! MOVE, O BLESSED BODY OF MINE!
FOR CHRIST, THE LIVING KING, HAS MUCH TO SAY DURING THIS PANDEMIC PERIOD OF TIME.

FOR HOLY AND TRUE-
ARE THE HEAVEN SENT WORDS THAT WILL SEE US THROUGH.

HOLY, HOLY, HOLY-
ARE THE LIVING WORDS OF CHRIST ALMIGHTY!!!

MOVE ME, O GREAT AND HOLY KING

BARBARA SPEAKING TO CHRIST, THE FOREVER-LIVING KING

Move me: move me:
move me, O holy King Almighty.

Move me in the direction of *your spiritually needy children.*
Move me in the direction of *your loved ones from every nation.*

Move me in the midst of *your divine love-*
Move me with the force and power of your divine love, *as it descends from sweet Heaven above.*

Move me with *great compassion-*
Move me in the direction of *your wandering creation.*

For *I desire, you see-*
To do the things that will *please God Almighty.*

Move me, *O great God and King-*
Move me in the midst of *your holy bells as they ring.*

For they do, *with silence ring-*
As I share the Heaven sent words of *Christ, my King.*

MOVE ME. MOVE ME. *MOVE ME, O GREAT AND HOLY ONE.* MOVE ME, O *KING JESUS,* WITH THE POWER THAT FLOWS FROM THE HOLY SPIRIT OF GOD, THE FATHER'S, ONLY BEGOTTEN SON.

FOR *I DESIRE, YOU SEE-* TO MOVE IN THE DIRECTION OF *THE CHILDREN WHO ARE CALLED AND CHOSEN BY CHRIST ALMIGHTY.*

ONLY YOU, *O LORD KING*

BARBARA SPEAKING TO *KING JESUS*

ONLY YOU, LORD KING JESUS-
HAVE THE DIVINE POWER AND GRACE TO *TAKE GOOD CARE OF US.*

FOR, *YOUR MAJESTY-*
REVEALS *YOUR HEAVENLY BEAUTY.*

YOU ALONE, *O LORD GOD-*
SHARE WITH YOUR EARTHLY LOVED ONES, *THE DEPTH OF YOUR REALM OF UNENDING LOVE.*

ONLY YOU-
REVEAL THE TRUTH SURROUNDING THE BLESSED ONE WHO IS HOLY, ETERNAL AND TRUE.

FOR *ONLY YOU-*
CAN SAVE THE WANDERING LOVED ONES WHO BELONG TO *THE EXISTING GOD WHO IS EVERLASTING AND TRUE.*

ONLY YOU-
ONLY YOU-
ONLY YOU-
CAN LEAD YOUR LOVED ONES THROUGH.

Through the *gates of sweet eternity*-
That are open to the blessed ones who *belong to God Almighty.*

Holy, holy, holy-
Are the gates the lead to *the only King called Christ Almighty!!!*

When will they learn, O great and holy King Jesus, that you are not a racist, and will not tolerate racism?

<u>Barbara speaking to the great and holy King Jesus</u>

When will they learn, *O great and holy God, King, and Creator*-
That you are the God and Father of *your earthly son and daughter?*

When will they learn, *O great and holy King of Kings*-
That you are *sovereign over every earthly people and things?*

When will they *understand*-
That you are *governor over every woman, child and man?*

When will they see-
That you are *the loving King and God, called Christ Almighty?*

WHEN WILL *THEY TAKE PART-*
IN INCLUDING THE HUMAN RACE *WITHIN THEIR GOD ORDERED COMPASSIONATE HEART?*

WHEN?
WHEN?
WHEN WITH THE PROFESSED CHRISTIANS *REMOVE THEMSELVES FROM RACISM AND PREJUDICE, WHICH IS A DEATH LEADING SIN?*

WHEN, DEAR LORD GOD, WHEN?
WHEN WILL *GODLY LOVE AND COMPASSION ON EARTH, BEGIN?*

DO NOT BE A PART OF THIS SINKING WORLD, *SAYS CHRIST, THE EVERLASTING KING*

<u>CHRIST, THE EVERLASTING KING, SPEAKING</u>

DEAR CHILDREN-
YES, YOU, *MY LOVED ONES FROM EVERY NATION!*

THIS WORLD OF YOURS IS *SINKING-*
FOR MANY *DO NOT FOLLOW THE HOLY WAY OF CHRIST, THE KING.*

THEY HAVE TURNED THEIR *DECEIVED BACKS ON ME.*
THEY HAVE BECOME *A FOLLOWER OF SATAN, MY ENEMY.*

FLEE FROM *THIS SINKING WORLD, DEAR CHILDREN!*
I AM CALLING OUT TO *THOSE WHO ARE MY CHOSEN.*

FOR *THE WORLD, YOU SEE-*
WORSHIPS *A GOD OTHER THAN ME.*

They do *the works and deeds of He-*
whom, in the past, *has turned His back on Me.*

Flee! Flee! Flee!
Flee to *the Holy King who will set you free!*

For the realm of *evil and destruction-*
has sought and stolen *many of My called children.*

Flee from the kingdom of destruction, *dear captive children of Mine*

<u>Christ, the Everlasting KING, Speaking</u>

Remove yourselves from *the kingdom of destruction, dear one.*
Show Satan, the ruler of that kingdom, that *you belong to God, the Father's, only begotten Son.*

For *Satan's kingdom of destruction-*
has *revealed its corruption.*

Flee from his harm-
and come to *your Creator's loving arm.*

Flee *Satan's realm of evil, dear ones-*
and join *My life seeking daughters and sons!*

For *Satan's realm of deception-*
will lead to *his kingdom's destruction.*

For *holy and true-*
is the eternal *King JESUS, who is calling out to you.*

CONE! COME! COME!
COME TO MY BLESSED KINGDOM!!!

FOR *IT GIVES EVERLASTING LIFE-*
TO *THE FAITHFUL HUSBAND AND WIFE.*

HOLY, HOLY, HOLY-
IS THE EVERLASTING KINGDOM OF GOD ALMIGHTY!!!

THE TWO KINGDOMS AND *THE TWO WORLDS*

CHRIST, THE EVERLASTING KING, SPEAKING

MY CHILDREN-
YES, *MY GREATEST CREATION.*

THERE ARE *TWO KINGDOMS, YOU SEE-*
AND ONE OF THEM *BELONGS TO ME.*

THERE ARE *TWO WORLDS THAT EXIST-*
AND ONE OF THEM, *I AM IN THE INHABITANTS MIDST.*

THERE ARE *TWO ROADS, YOU SEE-*
AND ONE OF THEM *LEADS TO THE HEAVENLY HOME OF GOD ALMIGHTY.*

THERE IS THE ROAD TO EVERLASTING LIFE, WHICH *I HAVE FORMED FOR MY FAITHFUL CREATION.*
AND THERE IS THE ROAD THAT *LEADS TO EVERLASTING DESTRUCTION.*

THERE IS A KINGDOM, *WHICH HAS NO KING.*
FOR THAT PLACE OF EXISTENCE *WREAKS OF AN EVIL THING.*

THERE IS A PLACE WHERE *EVERLASTING LIFE EXISTS-*
THERE IS A PLACE WHERE *KING JESUS IS IN HIS FAITHFUL SUBJECTS BLESSED MIDST.*

THERE IS *A SPIRITUAL WORLD OF FAME-*
WHERE *CHRIST JESUS IS ITS ONLY NAME.*

FOR *MY WORLD, YOU SEE-*
IS *RULED BY THE HOLY TRINITY.*

AND *MY KINGDOM, YOU SEE-*
IS INHABITED WITH *THE SUBJECTS WHO FOLLOW HOLY ME.*

THERE IS THE KINGDOM THAT IS *FULL OF DEATH AND DESTRUCTION-*
IT IS THE KINGDOM THAT *HOLDS THOSE WHO ARE NOT MY CHOSEN.*

FOR THE *KINGDOM OF DESTRUCTION-*
IS RULED BY *THE EVIL ONE (SATAN, THE DEVIL) AND HIS DEMONIC CREATION.*

FOR THE DEVIL'S *WORKS OF DESTRUCTION-*
CANNOT AND WILL NOT *CAPTURE MY OBEDIENT AND FAITHFUL CHILDREN.*

FOR *HOLY, YOU SEE-*
IS THE KINGDOM THAT IS RULED BY CHRIST ALMIGHTY.

HELP THEM, DEAR KING JESUS. PLEASE HELP THE LOST ONES

BARBARA SPEAKING TO KING JESUS

THEY ARE WALKING AROUND AS *THE SPIRITUALLY BLIND ONES.*
IN REALITY, THEY ARE *SATAN'S DECEIVED DAUGHTERS AND SONS.*

THEY ARE NOT AWARE, YOU SEE-
OF *THEIR FUTURE AND DESTINY.*

FOR THEIR *WORLDLY LIFESTYLES, YOU SEE-*
ARE THAT OF *SATAN'S, GOD'S ENEMY.*

THEY MOVE AS IF *NOTHING IS WRONG-*
AND THEY SHARE THEIR INNER CHARACTER *THROUGH THE WORDS IN THEIR POPULAR, BUT "UNHOLY" SONG.*

THEY WALK BLINDLY IN THE MIDST OF *SATAN'S DEAD END STREET-*
AS THEIR SONGS AND LYRICS *CONFUSE THOSE WHOM THEY GREET.*

FOR THE SPIRITUALLY *BLINDED ONES, YOU SEE-*
SPEAK AND SING SONGS THAT REVEAL THEIR CONNECTION AND ASSOCIATION WITH SATAN, *CHRIST, THE KING ALMIGHTY'S, ENEMY.*

HELP THE BLINDED ONES, *DEAR LORD GOD.*
HELP THEM BEFORE THEY DIE *WITHOUT KNOWING AND EXPERIENCING YOUR DIVINE LOVE.*

FOR *THEY TRULY DO-*
NEED HEAVEN SENT YOU.

HOLY, HOLY, HOLY-
IS THE HELP THAT COMES FROM CHRIST JESUS, THE ETERNAL KING AND GOD ALMIGHTY!!!

HELP YOUR BLINDED CHILDREN.
BEFORE SATAN DESTROYS *A GRIEVING AND VULNERABLE NATION.*

WHAT CAN I DO TO HELP, KING JESUS?

<u>BARBARA SPEAKING TO KING JESUS</u>

AS I GO BEFORE *CHRIST, THE FOREVER-LIVING KING-*
I ASK ONE IMPORTANT THING.

WHAT CAN I DO-
TO HELP LIFE SAVING YOU?

WHAT CAN I DO-
TO HELP BRING *THE LOST ONES TO YOU?*

TELL ME, KING JESUS.
TELL ME WHAT TO DO IN ORDER TO *WITNESS THE PRESENCE OF THE RIGHTEOUS.*

WHERE ARE THEY-
WHO FOLLOW YOUR LIFE REWARDING HOLY WAY?

LEAD ME. LEAD ME. LEAD ME.
LEAD ME TO THOSE WHO FOLLOW THE HOLY TEACHINGS OF CHRIST

ALMIGHTY.

FOR *I AM SEARCHING, YOU SEE-*
FOR *THE RIGHTEOUS CHILDREN OF GOD ALMIGHTY.*

SHOW ME, DEAR LORD GOD.
LEAD ME TO *YOUR CHILDREN OF DIVINE LOVE.*

FOR *I TRULY DESIRE TO SEE-*
THOSE WHO *BELIEVE IN SWEET ETERNITY (ALMIGHTY GOD).*

I WANT *TO WITNESS-*
THE *FAITHFUL ONES KINDNESS.*

FOR, *THE OTHER WORLD, YOU SEE-*
DOESN'T FOLLOW *THE HOLINESS OF CHRIST ALMIGHTY.*

I WANT TO BEHOLD-
THE LOVED ONES WHO WILL *WALK YOUR HEAVENLY STREETS OF GOLD.*

LEAD ME. LEAD ME.
LEAD ME TO THE CHOSEN LOVED ONES OF GOD ALMIGHTY.

BEFORE YOU LEAVE, SAYS CHRIST, THE KING

CHRIST, THE KING, SPEAKING

DEAR CHILDREN-
YES, YOU FROM EVERY NATION!

BEFORE YOU LEAVE THIS UNCERTAIN EARTH-
BE SURE THAT YOU ENTER YOUR SECOND BIRTH.

FOR YOUR LIMITED TIME HERE-
LEADS YOU TO AN UNENDING REALM THAT IS VERY NEAR.

DEAR SON AND DAUGHTER:
MAKE SURE THAT YOU FOLLOW THE ROAD THAT LEADS TO CHRIST JESUS, YOUR HEAVENLY KING AND FATHER.

MAKE SURE THAT YOU ARE ON THE PATH OF THE RIGHTEOUS-
MAKE SURE THAT YOU ARE WALKING IN THE FOOT PRINTS OF CHRIST JESUS.

PLEASE TAKE THE TIME, DEAR ONES-
FOR YOU ARE ONE OF KING JESUS' WORTHY AND SANCTIFIED DAUGHTERS AND SONS.

FOR THE ROAD AHEAD-
IS DESTINED FOR THE LIVING AND THE DEAD.

MAKE PEACE WITH CHRIST, THE EVERLASTING KING-
SO THAT YOUR ROAD AHEAD WILL LEAD YOU TO LIFE EVERLASTING.

FOR ONLY THE RIGHTEOUS, YOU SEE-
WILL LIVE FOREVER WITH ALMIGHTY GOD; SWEET ETERNITY.

DEAR CHILDREN-
O BLESSED CREATION:

WALK UPRIGHT-
FOR YOU ARE ALWAYS WITHIN MY SAVING SIGHT.

FOR *HOLY AND TRUE*-
IS THE KING AND GOD WHO *SEES HIS REPENTANT ONES THROUGH.*

HOLY, HOLY, HOLY-
IS THE KING AND GOD ALMIGHTY!!!

FOR *I AM IN YOUR MIDST*-
I AM THE HOLY KING WHO WILL FOREVER EXIST.

HOLY, HOLY, HOLY-
IS THE EXISTING GOD ALMIGHTY!!!

LONG LIVE THE KING!!!

BARBARA SPEAKING

KING JESUS LIVES FOREVER-
AND HE REIGNS IN OUR BLESSED MIDST WITH GOD, THE FATHER.

FOR HE IS IN THE MIDST, YOU SEE-
OF THOSE WHO ARE FAITHFUL TO THE ALMIGHTY.

LONG LIVE THE KING-
FOR HE HAS ENTERED EARTH WITH A WONDERFUL AND GLORIOUS THING.

HE COMES WITH THE DELIGHT-
THAT SHINES ON THE FAITHFUL ONES THROUGHOUT THE NIGHT.

HE COMES IN GLORY-
HE REVEALS THE DEPTHS OF HIS HOLY UNCHANGING STORY.

FOR KING JESUS, YOU SEE-
SURELY WALKS THROUGHOUT EACH DAY WITH BLESSED SENT ME.

THE KING IS TRULY ALIVE, YOU SEE-
FOR HE SPEAKS HIS HOLY WORDS OF SALVATION DIRECTLY TO ME.

FOR *HOLY AND TRUE-*
IS THE KING AND GOD WHO WALKS IN THE MIDST OF ME AND YOU.

LONG LIVE KING JESUS!
LONG LIVE THE HOLY ONE WHO SAVES US!!!

FOR *HE WALKS TODAY-*
IN THE MIDST OF THOSE WHO HAVE *SOUGHT HIS REWARDING HOLY WAY.*

HOLY, HOLY, HOLY-
IS THE LIVING CHRIST ALMIGHTY!!!

AS THE KING'S HEAVENLY GATES *OPEN WIDE FOR ME*

<u>BARBARA SPEAKING</u>

I WILL ENTER THE HEAVENLY GATES OF HE-
WHO RULES AND REIGNS OVER *HIS CHOSEN LOVED ONES AND BLESSED ME.*

I WILL *ENTER THE HEAVENLY GATES, YOU SEE-*
AND I WILL ENTER WITH *THE CHOSEN ONES WHO WERE FAITHFUL TO GOD ALMIGHTY.*

I WILL TAKE THEM BY *THEIR PRECIOUS HAND-*
AS I LEAD THEM TO *GOD'S HEAVENLY LAND.*

I WILL ENTER *THE KING'S HEAVENLY GATES WITH GLADNESS-*
AS HIS LOVED ONES AND I *EXPERIENCE HIS REALM OF HOLINESS.*

WE WILL WALK THROUGH *THE KING'S HEAVENLY GATES WITH BOLDNESS-*
AS WE GIVE HOMAGE AND THANKSGIVING *IN THE MIDST OF HIS GOODNESS.*

FOR *HOLY, YOU SEE-*
ARE THE HEAVENLY GATES THAT *LEAD TO THE THRONE OF CHRIST ALMIGHTY.*

WE WILL ENTER-
AND WE WILL GREET *GOD, OUR HEAVENLY FATHER.*

FOR *HE DESIRES, YOU SEE-*
TO BEHOLD THE CHILDREN WHO ARE *CALLED AND CHOSEN BY HE.*

OPEN WIDE, *O BLESSED GATES OF CHRIST, THE HOLY KING!*
OPEN WIDE, SO THAT WE MAY *BEHOLD KING JESUS' DIVINITY AND MAJESTY!!!*

LET THE HEAVENLY RESIDENTS *ANNOUNCE US-*
LET THE INSTRUMENTS SOUND *AS WE APPROACH THE MIGHTY THRONE OF KING JESUS!!!*

FOR *HOLY AND REAL-*
IS THE KING'S PRESENCE THAT *THE CHOSEN ONES CAN SURELY FEEL.*

HOLY, HOLY, HOLY-
IS THE PRESENCE OF THE KING ALMIGHTY!!!

SATAN, THE DEVIL, *DOESN'T DISCRIMINATE*

CHRIST, THE KING, SPEAKING

HE, SATAN, *DOESN'T DISCRIMINATE, YOU SEE-*
FOR HE TAKES DOWN *EVERYONE WHO DOESN'T FOLLOW HOLY ME.*

HE SEEKS *THOSE WHOM I CALL-*
SO THAT THEY WILL *EXPERIENCE DESTRUCTION AND PAIN WHEN THEY FALL.*

HE ISN'T CHOOSY-
HE GOES AFTER *THE BRILLIANT ONES AND THE LOWLY.*

HE SEEKS, YOU SEE-
EVERYONE WHO ISN'T CAPTURED BY *THE LOVE OF ME; GOD ALMIGHTY.*

FOR *HIS DESIRE-*
IS TO TAKE ALL OF MY CHILDREN WITH HIM, *AS HE ENTERS THE GATES THAT LEAD TO DESTRUCTION AND EVERLASTING FIRE.*

FOR HE IS *THE "UNHOLY ONE"-*
WHO SEEKS TO *DESTROY EVERY DAUGHTER AND SON.*

HE IS *THE REALM OF DOOM, YOU SEE-*
FOR HE IS *SATAN, MY ENEMY.*

BE AWARE, DEAR CHILDREN-
THAT SATAN DOESN'T DISCRIMINATE WHEN IT COMES TO *DESTROYING MY GREATEST CREATION.*

FLEE FROM HIS EVIL WAYS-
FOR HE CAPTURES *THE ONE WHO STRAYS.*

THE KING IS SEATED *IN THE MIDST OF THE REPENTANT ONES*

<u>CHRIST, THE KING, SPEAKING</u>

I HAVE SEATED MYSELF, YOU SEE-
IN THE PRESENCE OF *THOSE WHO COME BEFORE ME.*

I HAVE SEATED MYSELF *IN THE MIDST OF THE REPENTANT ONES,*
AND I WILL GLADLY *FORGIVE MY OBEDIENT DAUGHTERS AND SONS.*

FOR *THEY DID FLEE, YOU SEE-*
FROM THE REALM OF EVIL THAT IS *GOVERNED BY SATAN, MY ENEMY.*

I HAVE PLACED MYSELF IN THE PRESENCE OF THOSE WHO DID *SEEK MY REALM THAT HOLDS THE RIGHTEOUS.*
I HAVE PLACED MYSELF IN THE MIDST OF THE REPENTANT ONES WHO *LONG FOR THE HOLY REALM OF KING JESUS.*

FOR *HOLY AND TRUE-*
IS THE KING WHO HAS FORGIVEN YOU.

YOU HAVE COME BEFORE *MY THRONE OF FORGIVENESS-*
AND NOW, YOU WILL *WITNESS MY GLORY AND HOLINESS.*

FOR *HOLY AND TRUE-*
IS THE KING AND GOD WHO HAS *FORGIVEN REPENTANT YOU.*

HOLY, HOLY, HOLY-
IS THE FORGIVING CHRIST ALMIGHTY.

WHERE WILL YOU GO AFTER YOU LEAVE ME, SAYS CHRIST, THE EVERLASTING KING

CHRIST, THE EVERLASTING KING, SPEAKING

DEAR CHILDREN-
FROM EVERY NATION.

WHERE WILL YOU GO AFTER YOU LEAVE ME?
WHERE IS YOUR DESTINY?

FOR YOU DID NOT BELIEVE-
THE HOLY WORDS FROM ME THAT YOU WOULD NOT RECEIVE.

WHERE IS YOUR FINAL DESTINATION?
WILL YOU BE A PART OF MY GREAT CELEBRATION?

FOR THE CHOSEN ONES, YOU SEE-
WILL CELEBRATE THROUGHOUT SWEET ETERNITY WITH ME.

WHAT IS YOUR FATE?
AFTER MY JUDGMENT DAY, WILL YOU ENTER MY HEAVENLY GATE?

WHERE WILL YOU GO, DEAR ONE?
WILL YOU ENTER THE HEAVENLY HOME OF GOD, OUR FATHER'S, ONLY BEGOTTEN SON?

WHERE WILL YOU SPEND ETERNITY?
WILL IT BE WITH SWEET ETERNITY; GOD ALMIGHTY?

WHERE WILL YOU GO? WHERE WILL YOU GO? WHERE WILL YOU GO AFTER YOU LEAVE ME?
WILL YOU SHARE THE MIGHTY THRONE *WITH CHRIST ALMIGHTY?*

FOR *HOLY AND TRUE-*
IS THE KING WHO WILL JUDGE YOU!!!

THEY WILL NOT ENTER HEAVEN'S GATES, *SAYS CHRIST JESUS, THE LOVING KING*

<u>CHRIST, THE EVERLASTING KING, SPEAKING</u>

THOSE WHO *COMMIT SIN-*
WILL NOT BE *INVITED IN.*

FOR *ONLY THE RIGHTEOUS-*
WILL BE PERMITTED TO *DWELL IN SWEET HEAVEN WITH GOD, THE FATHER, AND KING JESUS.*

FOR *THE UNREPENTANT SINNER, YOU SEE-*
WILL NOT BE *INVITED BY ME.*

FOR *THE UNHOLY ONES-*
ARE NOT *MY WORTHY DAUGHTERS AND SONS.*

THEY HAVE *CHOSEN, YOU SEE-*
THEIR *EVERLASTING DESTINY.*

I WILL *NOT WEEP FOR THEM, YOU SEE-*
FOR THEY DID *TURN THEIR BACKS ON ME.*

LIVE FOR ME: *LIVE FOR THE GREAT AND HOLY KING AND GOD ALMIGHTY*

CHRIST, THE EVERLASTING KING, SPEAKING

O BLESSED ONES-
OH *MY BELOVED DAUGHTERS AND SONS!*

LIVE RIGHT FOR ME.
LIVE RIGHT IN *THE HOLY EYES OF THE KING ALMIGHTY.*

FOR *I DO DESIRE, YOU SEE-*
THAT YOU *DWELL THROUGHOUT SWEET ETERNITY WITH ME.*

FOR *HOLY, YOU SEE-*
ARE THE BLESSED AND CHOSEN ONES WHO WILL *ENTER SWEET HEAVEN WITH ETERNAL ME.*

FOR *HOLY AND TRUE-*
IS THE KING WHO *SPEAKS EVERY DAY TO BLESSED AND BELOVED YOU.*

HOLY, HOLY, HOLY-
IS THE FOREVER-LIVING *CHRIST ALMIGHTY!!!*

THE DIVINE KING SITS

BARBARA SPEAKING

CHRIST JESUS-
IS THE DIVINE KING WHO *SITS IN THE MIDST OF US.*

HIS MIGHTY THRONE, YOU SEE-
SITS IN THE MIDST OF YOU AND ME.

FOR *HOLY, YOU SEE-*
IS THE GREAT GOD AND KING, *CHRIST ALMIGHTY.*

FOR TODAY, *WITHIN OUR BLESSED MIDST-*
THE HOLY SPIRIT OF CHRIST, THE KING, *DOES EXIST.*

YES! *THE HEAVENLY KING, YOU SEE-*
SITS ON HIS MIGHTY THRONE IN THE MIDST OF YOU AND ME.

OH WHAT *A DIVINE SIGHT-*
TO WITNESS THE KING'S MAJESTY *THROUGHOUT THIS VERY DARK NIGHT.*

FOR *HOLY AND TRUE-*
IS THE MIGHTY *THRONE OF KING JESUS THAT SEES HIS LOVED ONES THROUGH.*

FOR THE HOLY KING'S *THRONE OF LOVE, YOU SEE-*
DOES SIT IN THE MIDST OF *YOU AND ME.*

I WILL WAIT AND SEE-
THE BLESSINGS THAT *FALL FROM THE THRONE OF CHRIST ALMIGHTY.*

FOR *HOLY AND TRUE-*
IS THE THRONE THAT SITS IN THE MIDST OF ME AND YOU.

HOLY, HOLY, HOLY-
IS THE THRONE OF CHRIST ALMIGHTY!!!

AS CHRIST, THE HEAVENLY KING, RISES FROM HIS HOLY THRONE ON HIGH

BARBARA SPEAKING

AS THE HOLY KING *RISES FROM HIS HOLY THRONE ON HIGH-*
I BOW IN THE PRESENCE OF *THE GREAT ONE WHO HAS COME TO SAVE YOU AND I.*

AS THE HOLY KING *RISES FROM HIS MIGHTY THRONE OF LOVE-*
MY BLESSED SPIRIT BOWS IN THE PRESENCE OF THE DIVINE KING WHO *ROSE FROM HIS HEAVENLY THRONE ABOVE.*

FOR *KING JESUS, YOU SEE-*
NOW *WALKS IN THE MIDST OF YOU AND ME.*

FOR *HIS MIGHTY THRONE ON HIGH-*
SITS IN THE MIDST: *YES! ABOVE THE BRIGHT BLUE SKY.*

HE LOOKS AROUND, YOU SEE-
AS *HE GAZES IN THE DIRECTION OF BLESSED ME.*

FOR *HE LOOKS TO SEE-*
THE BLESSED ONE WHO *FOLLOWED THE FOREVER-LIVING KING; CHRIST ALMIGHTY.*

HOLY, HOLY, HOLY-
IS THE HEAVENLY THRONE OF GOD ALMIGHTY!!!

FOR IN *OUR BLESSED PRESENCE-*
WALKS THE HOLY SPIRIT OF ALMIGHTY GOD; *SWEET EXISTENCE.*

BARBARA SPEAKING TO KING JESUS

COME, O BLESSED ONE!
RELEASE YOUR GOODNESS IN THE PRESENCE OF *YOUR DAUGHTER AND SON.*

FOR *WE DESIRE TO SEE-*
THE HOLY HEAVENLY KING CALLED *CHRIST JESUS, THE ALMIGHTY.*

HOLY, HOLY, HOLY AND REAL-
IS THE PRESENCE OF THE KING'S THRONE THAT I CAN TRULY SEE AND FEEL.

FOR THE LOVE OF *CHRIST, THE KING*

BARBARA SPEAKING

FOR THE LOVE OF MY HOLY GOD AND SAVIOR, *CHRIST, THE FOREVER-LIVING KING-*
I WILL DO THE GOOD WORKS OF *HE WHO TAKES VERY GOOD CARE OF HIS BLESSED ONES EVERYTHING.*

FOR *KING JESUS, YOU SEE-*
REALLY LOVES THE CHILDREN WHO ARE *CALLED AND CHOSEN BY HOLY ETERNAL HE.*

FOR THE LOVE OF *OUR ETERNAL GOD AND KING; CHRIST JESUS-*
I WILL BOW IN THE PRESENCE OF THE MIGHTY KING, WHO *WALKS WITH US IN THE MIDST OF THE DEVASTATION THAT COMES WITH THE CORONAVIRUS.*

FOR *HOLY AND REAL-*
IS THE PRESENCE OF CHRIST, THE KING, THAT *HIS LOVING CHILDREN TODAY, CAN TRULY FEEL.*

HOLY, HOLY, HOLY-
IS OUR GREAT KING; CHRIST ALMIGHTY!!!

LET HEAVEN AND EARTH *BOW IN THE HOLY PRESENCE OF CHRIST JESUS, THE KING*

BARBARA SPEAKING

BOW! BOW! BOW!
LET HEAVEN AND EARTH *SHOW HOMAGE AND RESPECT TO CHRIST, THE FOREVER-LIVING KING, RIGHT NOW!*

FOR *HE RULES! HE RULES! HE RULES, YOU SEE-*
HE RULES IN THE MIDST AND PRESENCE OF *HEAVEN, EARTH, AND ME!*

HE IS *THE MIGHTY KING ON HIGH-*
HE DESERVES TO BE *ACKNOWLEDGED BY YOU AND I.*

FOR CHRIST, THE FOREVER REIGNING KING, *YOU SEE-*
MOVES IN THE MIDST AND PRESENCE OF *SWEET HEAVEN AND ME.*

HOLY, HOLY, HOLY-
IS THE PRESENCE OF CHRIST *JESUS, THE ALMIGHTY!!!*

SINGING WITH CHRIST, THE HEAVEN SENT *KING, IN THE MIDST OF MY MANY SPIRITUAL AND PHYSICAL STORMS*

BARBARA SPEAKING

I LIFT MY BLESSED VOICE IN *MY EARTHLY RESIDENCE-*
AS I SING TO *CHRIST, THE KING, IN HIS HOLY PRESENCE.*

I SING *SONGS OF ELATION AND JOY-*
AS I SING WITH THE KING WHO *RULES AND REIGNS OVER EVERY TRUSTING GIRL AND BOY.*

I SING SONGS OF PRAISE OUT LOUD-
IN THE MIDST OF *THE HOLY REALM THAT MAKES ME PROUD.*

FOR *KING JESUS, YOU SEE-*
IS PROUD OF ME.

HALLELUJAH! HALLELUJAH-
TO *THE HOLY ETERNAL SON OF GOD, THE FATHER, JEHOVAH!!!*

CELEBRATE, FOR *CHRIST, THE* KING, *HAS ARRIVED*

BARBARA SPEAKING

HE HAS ARRIVED! HE HAS ARRIVED! CHRIST JESUS, OUR GLORIOUS KING, NOW, IS IN OUR MIDST-
AND HIS GLORIOUS WORKS AMONG US REVEAL THAT *HE DOES EXIST.*

HE HAS ARRIVED WITH *GREAT MIGHT AND POWER-*
THAT HE SHINES ON US *EVERY BLESSED SECOND, MINUTE AND HOUR.*

FOR *CHRIST, THE HEAVENLY KING-*
HAS ARRIVED WITH *A GLORIOUS THING.*

HALLELUJAH! HALLELUJAH! HALLELUJAH!
TO *THE MIGHTY SON OF* JEHOVAH!!!

HE HAS ARRIVED, AND *HE DWELLS IN THE MIDST OF US.*
WE ARE BLESSED WITH *THE HOLY PRESENCE OF KING* JESUS.

HE WALKS IN OUR MIDST TODAY-
AND *I WILL SHOUT* HALLELUJAH *AS I FOLLOW HIS LIFE SAVING HOLY WAY.*

FOR *HOLY AND TRUE-*
IS THE HEAVENLY KING WHO *NOW DWELLS IN THE MIDST OF ME AND YOU.*

HOLY, HOLY, HOLY-
IS THE VISIBLE REIGNING CHRIST ALMIGHTY!!!

HE HAS ARRIVED, DEAR ONES-
AND HE WALKS IN THE MIDST OF HIS NEEDY DAUGHTERS AND SONS!

AND HE, CHRIST JESUS, CONTINUES TO REIGN

BARBARA SPEAKING

CHRIST, THE FOREVER LIVING KING, DOES REIGN-
AND HE RULES IN THE MIDST OF *THIS WORLD'S CONTINUOUS PAIN.*

HE RULES FROM *HIS MIGHTY THRONE OF HIGH-*
AS HE SENDS DOWN *HIS HEAVENLY BLESSINGS TO YOU AND I.*

HE RULES FROM *HIS MIGHTY THRONE ABOVE-*
AS HE RELEASES IN OUR MIDST, *HIS EVER-FLOWING BASKET OF LOVE.*

FOR *HOLY AND TRUE-*
IS THE KING WHO *RULES IN THE MIDST OF ME AND YOU.*

HE REIGNS *OVER THE BLESSED ONES-*
AND HE SPEAKS SOFTLY AND PATIENTLY *TO HIS WORTHY AND WELL-LOVED DAUGHTERS AND SONS.*

FOR *HOLY AND TRUE-*
IS THE REIGNING KING WHO *LOVES ME AND YOU.*

HOLY, HOLY, HOLY-
IS THE REIGNING KING, CALLED CHRIST ALMIGHTY!!!

FOR CHRIST JESUS, THE HEAVEN SENT KING, STILL RULES OVER HIS LOVED ONES ON EARTH

BARBARA SPEAKING

KING JESUS-
STILL RULES AND REIGNS OVER US.

EVEN IN OUR BLESSED MIDST-
HE DOES EXIST.

HE EXISTS IN THE MIDST OF US-
FOR WE ARE THE LOVED ONES OF KING JESUS.

HE RULES IN THE MIDST OF HIS LOVES ONES-
AND HE REIGNS IN THE MIDST OF HIS BLESSED DAUGHTERS AND SONS.

FOR HOLY AND TRUE-
IS THE KING WHO REIGNS AND RULES OVER ME AND YOU.

THE KING HAS CHOSEN ME TO SERVE HIS NEEDY LOVED ONES

BARBARA SPEAKING

I HAVE BEEN CHOSEN-
TO HONOR AND SERVE CHRIST, THE KING'S, EARTHLY CHILDREN.

HE HAS SENT ME-
TO DELIVER THE SPIRITUAL FOOD THAT COMES FROM GOD ALMIGHTY.

I HAVE BEEN *SENT BY HE-*
WHO SITS ON HIS HEAVENLY THRONE *NEXT TO JEHOVAH* GOD ALMIGHTY.

FOR *HOLY AND TRUE-*
IS THE KING WHO HAS *SENT ME TO YOU.*

I HAVE BEEN SENT *TO SERVE THE RICH AND THE POOR.*
I HAVE BEEN SENT TO *OPEN GOD'S HOLY DOOR.*

FOR *HIS HOLY DOOR LEADS-*
TO HIS EARTHLY LOVED ONES *WHOM HE FEEDS.*

FOR *HIS HEAVEN SENT KNOWLEDGE, YOU SEE-*
IS THE SPIRITUAL FOOD THAT *THE KING FEEDS YOU AND ME.*

HOLY, HOLY, HOLY-
IS THE HEAVEN SENT FOOD THAT COMES FROM THE KING ALMIGHTY!!!

FOR HIS BASKET OF HOLY WORDS THAT ARE *FILLED WITH DIVINE LOVE-*
COMES FROM *THE GENEROSITY OF OUR HOLY HEAVENLY GOD.*

HOLY, HOLY, HOLY-
IS OUR ETERNAL GOD ALMIGHTY!!!

IN THE HOLY PRESENCE OF CHRIST, THE KING, *I WILL SERVE*

<u>BARBARA SPEAKING</u>

I WILL *SERVE CHRIST, THE KING'S, INVITED GUESTS, YOU SEE-*
AS *HE SENDS THEM TO ME.*

I WILL SERVE THEM *IN THE MIDST OF THE CORONAVIRUS-*
AS I GIVE PRAISE TO *THE FOREVER RULER, GOD, AND KING,*
CHRIST JESUS.

FOR HE HAS SENT ME *TO SERVE HIS CHILDREN-*
WITH THE KNOWLEDGE THAT *DESCENDS TO ME FROM SWEET HEAVEN.*

I WILL SERVE *HIS INVITED GUESTS, YOU SEE-*
WITH THE SPIRITUAL NOURISHING FOOD THAT *HE SENDS DOWN TO ME.*

FOR *HOLY AND TRUE-*
IS THE FOOD THAT *KING* JESUS *SENDS TO ME AND YOU.*

SALUTING CHRIST JESUS, *THE FOREVER RULING AND REIGNING KING, TODAY*

BARBARA SPEAKING TO KING JESUS

I SALUTE YOU.
I SALUTE THE MIGHTY HEAVENLY KING, WHO IS *HOLY, ETERNAL AND TRUE.*

I SALUTE YOU, KING JESUS.
I SALUTE THE HEAVEN SENT KING WHO *DIED ON HIS CROSS OF LOVE, IN ORDER TO SAVE US.*

FOR *HOLY, EVERLASTING AND TRUE-*
IS THE GREAT REIGNING KING *WHO SEES HIS LOVED ONES THROUGH.*

FOR HE SEES US *THROUGH OUR ROUGH TIMES, YOU SEE-*
AND HE CONTINUOUSLY *HELPS THE CHILDREN WHO ARE CALLED BY GOD ALMIGHTY.*

I BOW IN *THE PRESENCE OF HE-*
WHO *DWELLS IN THE MIDST AND PRESENCE OF ETERNITY.*

HOLY, HOLY, HOLY-
IS OUR LORD, GOD, AND SAVIOR; CHRIST ALMIGHTY!!!

FOR *HE IS EVERLASTING-*
HE IS THE ETERNAL KING.

I WILL SALUTE AND GREET-
THE HOLY HEAVENLY KING WHOM *THE BLESSED ONES SEEK.*

CHRIST JESUS, THE HOLY HEAVENLY KING AND I ARE ONE

<u>BARBARA SPEAKING</u>

FUSED AND UNITED, YOU SEE-
ARE THE BLESSED SPIRITS OF *CHRIST ALMIGHTY AND ME.*

FOR BEFORE THE REALM OF *EXISTING TIME-*
CHRIST JESUS, THE HOLY HEAVENLY KING, *SAID THAT HE IS MINE.*

OH HOW *I DO TREASURE, YOU SEE-*
THE DIVINE UNITY OF *THE HOLY KING AND ME.*

FOR *BEFORE MY PHYSICAL BIRTH-*
CHRIST JESUS ENTERED THIS NEEDY EARTH.

BEFORE *THE EXISTENCE OF TIME, YOU SEE-*
CHRIST *JESUS,* THE HOLY HEAVENLY KING, *DECIDED TO UNITE WITH HIS EARTHLY CHILDREN AND ME.*

FOR *HOLY AND REAL-*
IS OUR UNION THAT *MY BLESSED SOUL CAN TRULY FEEL.*

FOR IT IS *A HEAVENLY UNION, YOU SEE-*
THAT IS *APPROVED BY GOD, THE FATHER;* YES, JEHOVAH, THE ALMIGHTY.

HOLY, HOLY, HOLY-
IS OUR UNITY!!!

FOR *I CANNOT MOVE AN INCH, YOU SEE-*
WITHOUT THE APPROVAL AND GUIDANCE OF *CHRIST, THE KING ALMIGHTY.*

HOLY, HOLY, HOLY-
IS OUR FOREVER-LIVING KING, CHRIST ALMIGHTY!!!

THE GREAT AND HOLY KING HAS RELEASED HIS BASKET FILLED WITH GOOD THINGS

<u>BARBARA SPEAKING</u>

I WILL CATCH IT!
I WILL RECEIVE *THE BLESSINGS FROM THE KING'S HOLY SPIRIT!*

I WILL CATCH *THE HEAVEN SENT GOOD THINGS-*
THAT DESCENDED TO ME FROM *CHRIST* JESUS, *THE KING OF KINGS.*

FOR *HIS DIVINE BASKET OF GOODNESS-*
IS FILLED WITH *HIS GLORY AND HOLINESS.*

YES! *CHRIST, THE FOREVER-LIVING KING OF KINGS-*
HAS SENT TO EARTH'S BLESSED INHABITANTS, *MANY GOOD AND BENEFICIAL THINGS.*

FOR *HOLY AND TRUE-*
ARE THE GOOD *HEAVENLY THINGS THAT ARE SENT TO ME AND YOU.*

HOLY, HOLY, HOLY-
ARE THE HEAVEN SENT BLESSINGS FROM GOD ALMIGHTY.

IN THE MIDST OF CELEBRATING THANKSGIVING, *I GIVE PRAISE TO CHRIST JESUS, OUR HEAVENLY KING*

<u>BARBARA SPEAKING</u>

IN THE MIDST OF CELEBRATING –
TO KING *JESUS, I OFFER MY THANKSGIVING.*

FOR *I AM CELEBRATING-*
THE REALITY OF *CHRIST, OUR FOREVER-LIVING REIGNING KING.*

OH HOW *GRATEFUL WE ARE-*
FOR WE GIVE THANKS TO *THE HOLY KING WHO ISN'T VERY FAR.*

HOLY, HOLY, HOLY-
IS OUR KING, CHRIST ALMIGHTY!!!

HOLY, HOLY, HOLY-
IS THE THANKSGIVING THAT I GIVE TO CHRIST ALMIGHTY!!!

FOR *HE DOES REIGN-*
IN THE MIDST OF *EARTH'S INHABITANTS PAIN.*

WHEN CHRIST, THE KING, WHISPERS TO MY SOUL, *MY BLESSED SPIRIT BOWS*

BARBARA SPEAKING TO KING JESUS

I CAN HEAR YOUR LOVELY HEAVEN SENT WHISPERS, *O GREAT AND HOLY KING.*
I CAN TRULY HEAR *EVERY BLESSED THING.*

FOR *YOUR HEAVENLY WHISPERS, YOU SEE-*
PENETRATE *THE MIND, BODY AND SOUL THAT BELONG TO BLESSED ME.*

YOU HAVE WHISPERED *YOUR WORDS OF DIVINE LOVE AND PEACE THROUGH THE MANY YEARS.*
YOU HAVE WHISPERED TO ME, O GREAT KING, *EVEN IN THE MIDST OF MY FALLING TEARS.*

YOUR HOLY WHISPERS WERE *AS MELODIOUS HEAVENLY SONGS TO ME.*
YOUR WHISPERS, O GREAT KING, *DID SET MY TORMENTED SOUL FREE.*

YOU WHISPERED TO ME *THROUGHOUT EACH DAY-*
WHICH LED MY NEEDY SOUL TO *BOW DOWN AND PRAY.*

YOUR HOLY WHISPERS *GAVE ME GREAT COMFORT AND JOY-*
IT GAVE ME THE PEACE THAT *THE WORLD CAN NEVER DESTROY.*

Your whispers are like *a great shining light-*
that brings peace to my soul *throughout the dark night.*

Oh how grateful-
to be *loved by a king who is eternal and wonderful.*

For *holy and true-*
are the peace, joy and comfort that *I experience from blessed you.*

Holy, holy, holy-
are the whispers that come from the spirit of our king almighty!!!

For my blessed spirit *dances, you see-*
as *king Jesus, whispers his melodious words of love and comfort to blessed and obedient me.*

Holy, holy, holy-
is the forever reigning God almighty!!!

The joy of being in *the holy presence of Christ, the King*

<u>Barbara speaking</u>

The joy! The joy! The great and holy joy!
It is a lovely heaven sent feeling that *the world and satan cannot destroy!*

For *Christ Jesus, my forever-reigning king-*
really loves to see me *dance and sing.*

I DANCE AND SING *IN THE KING'S HOLY PRESENCE.*
YES! I DANCE AND SING CONTINUOUSLY *WITHIN MY EARTHLY HOME AND RESIDENCE.*

FOR *THE JOY THAT HE BRINGS-*
CAN ONLY COME WITH THE LOVE THAT I HAVE FOR *CHRIST JESUS, THE FOREVER REIGNING KING OF KINGS.*

FOR THE JOY OF *BEING IN HIS HOLY PRESENCE-*
COMES FROM *HIS DAUGHTER WHO SHARES IN THE REVELATION OF HIS EXISTENCE.*

FOR *HOLY AND TRUE-*
IS THE JOY THAT I HAVE, AS *I BOW IN THE PRESENCE OF THE KING WHO RULES OVER BLESSED ME AND YOU.*

HOLY, HOLY, HOLY-
IS THE FOREVER REIGNING CHRIST ALMIGHTY!!!

WHEN KING JESUS SPEAKS TO ME, *MY ENTIRE BEING JUMPS FOR JOY*

<u>BARBARA SPEAKING</u>

MY BEATING HEART *JUMPS FOR JOY-*
WHENEVER I AM IN THE HOLY PRESENCE OF *THE KING WHO RULES OVER EVERY EARTHLY GIRL AND BOY.*

FOR *KING JESUS, YOU SEE-*
TRULY *RULES OVER BLESSED YOU AND ME.*

Beat, O blessed heart of mine!
Rejoice in the presence of holiness (King Jesus) throughout this period of time!

For King Jesus, you see-
has come to rescue you and me.

He will set us free-
from the sins that offend and hurt holy eternal He.

For His desire, you see-
is to walk, sing, and dance with purified you and me.

He will rescue-
the loved ones who belong to the great and holy King who is eternal and true.

Speak to me, O great and holy King, for I am in the presence of Your realm of holiness.
Speak to me, King Jesus, as I rejoice in the midst of Your goodness.

There are so many, Lord Jesus: many lost souls

<u>**Barbara speaking to King Jesus**</u>

There are many-
who do not follow the love and holy teachings of Christ Almighty.

It is unbelievable, but true-
that there are many who do not follow the holy words that come from You.

THEY SPEAK YOUR HOLY NAME *AS IF THEY KNOW YOU.*
BUT THEIR DAILY ACTS *REVEAL THEIR INNER BELIEF TOWARDS THE KING WHO IS ETERNAL AND TRUE.*

I SHAKE MY HEAD *WITH DISBELIEF,*
AND ONLY *KNOWING YOU GIVE ME RELIEF.*

FOR *THE LOST SOULS THAT I SEE-*
ARE FAR AWAY FROM THE COMMANDS THAT *YOU HAVE GIVEN TO YOUR LOVED ONES AND ME.*

FOR *HOLY, EVERLASTING AND TRUE-*
ARE *THE COMMANDMENTS THAT CAME FROM YOU.*

TO YOU, *KING* JESUS, *I OFFER MY GRATITUDE-*
FOR YOU HAVE *INCLUDED ME IN THE CELEBRATION WITH YOUR HEAVENLY MULTITUDE.*

FOR *HOLY AND TRUE-*
IS MY GRATITUDE TOWARDS *LIFE SAVING AND REWARDING YOU.*

HOLY, HOLY, HOLY-
IS THE FOREVER-LIVING KING ALMIGHTY!!!

DO THEY KNOW, *O GREAT AND HOLY* KING?

<u>BARBARA SPEAKING TO</u> KING JESUS

DO THEY KNOW, KING JESUS?
DO THEY KNOW THAT *YOU ARE THE ONLY WAY TO THE LAND OF THE RIGHTEOUS?*

DO THEY KNOW THAT YOU ARE THE ONLY PATH TO SWEET ETERNITY?
DO THEY KNOW THAT YOU ARE THE ONLY BEGOTTEN SON OF JEHOVAH GOD, THE ALMIGHTY?

DO THEY UNDERSTAND-
THAT YOU, O HOLY KING, ARE THE ONLY WAY TO HEAVEN'S PROMISED LAND?

I WILL TELL THEM, O GREAT AND HOLY LORD GOD.
I WILL TELL OF THE ONLY WAY TO THE FATHER'S REALM OF DIVINE LOVE.

I WILL TELL THEM YOUR TRUTH-
FOR YOU REVEALED IT TO ME WHILE IN MY YOUTH.

I WILL SHARE WITH YOUR LOVED ONES EVERYDAY-
THAT ETERNAL LIFE WITH YOU IS THE ONLY DESTINATION AND WAY.

FOR HOLY AND TRUE-
IS THE WAY THAT LEADS TO ETERNAL YOU.

HOLY, HOLY, HOLY-
IS THE ONLY ROAD THAT LEADS TO CHRIST, THE FOREVER LIVING KING ALMIGHTY!!!

FOR I WILL SPEAK-
THE HOLY WORDS THAT YOU GIVE TO ME TO SHARE WITH THE STRONG AND THE MEEK.

MY GOD: MY KING

BARBARA SPEAKING TO CHRIST, THE KING

O HOLY GOD AND KING-
I WANT TO BE A PART OF THE JUSTICE AND LOVE THAT YOUR HOLY SPIRIT AND POWER BRING.

I WANT TO WITNESS KING JESUS-
AND THE REALITY OF YOUR DIVINITY, AS YOU WALK IN THE MIDST OF US-

FOR YOUR HOLY PRESENCE AND GLORY-
ARE REVEALED TO THE LOVED ONES WHO HAVE WITNESSED AND BELIEVED IN YOUR DIVINITY.

O HOLY GOD- O BELOVED KING-
I HAVE FOLLOWED YOUR REALM THAT PIERCED EARTH'S INHABITANTS REALM OF EXISTENCE, AS THE REJOICING ONES DID SING.

YOU ARE THE TRUE DIVINE RULER TODAY-
EVEN AMONG THOSE WHO DO NOT BELIEVE OR FOLLOW YOUR LIFE REWARDING HOLY WAY.

FOR YOUR REALM OF GOODNESS, YOU SEE-
HAS CAPTURED BELIEVING ME.

HOLY, HOLY, HOLY-
IS MY LORD GOD, AND KING ALMIGHTY!!!

AT THE SOUND OF *THE HOLY KING'S NAME*

BARBARA SPEAKING TO KING JESUS

AT THE SOUND OF *YOUR HOLY NAME, KING JESUS-*
MY INNER FEARS REST WITHIN *THE GATES THAT LEAD TO THE HEAVENLY HOME OF THE VICTORIOUS KING WHO SAVES US.*

BARBARA SPEAKING OF KING JESUS

AT THE SOUND OF *HIS HOLY SPIRIT AND NAME-*
MY BLESSED SPIRIT *ENTERS HIS REALM OF DIVINE FAME.*

FOR *HOLY AND TRUE-*
IS THE NAME OF THE KING WHO HAS *SAVED ME AND YOU.*

HOLY, HOLY, HOLY-
IS THE ETERNAL NAME OF CHRIST, THE KING; THE ALMIGHTY!!!

KING JESUS, THE REALM OF DIVINE HOPE, *HAS ENTERED EARTH'S NEEDY*

BARBARA SPEAKING TO KING JESUS

WELCOME! WELCOME! WELCOME!
THANK YOU, KING JESUS, *FOR ENTERING YOUR EARTHLY KINGDOM!*

FOR WE ARE *IN NEED TODAY-*
OF *YOUR HOLY LIFE SAVING WAY.*

Welcome into our needy land.
We welcome *your powerful life rewarding hand.*

For *only you-*
can *see your earthly loved ones through.*

We welcome *your Holy Spirit of life and love-*
as you *descend to us from sweet Heaven above.*

We welcome *your guidance-*
as we *behold the works of your Holy presence.*

Welcome! Welcome! Welcome! Welcome, O great and mighty King of Kings!
We look forward to *receiving your Heavenly blessings!*

Holy, holy, holy-
is our hope in Christ Jesus; *God Almighty!!!*

My hope is in *the forever reigning* King Jesus

Barbara Speaking

I place *all of my hope and trust, you see-*
in the Heaven sent *King who reigns over you and me.*

King Jesus-
rules over blessed us.

He is my living hope-
He is the Holy Heavenly King who *helps His earthly loved ones cope.*

For in the midst of *hardship and pain-*
King *Jesus* will always rule and reign.

Oh what *a loving and thoughtful King-*
Who makes my blessed and appreciative soul *dance and sing.*

For *he lets me know-*
That *he is with me wherever my family, friends, and I go.*

Holy, holy, holy-
Is my love and hope in Christ Almighty!!!

For *he rules, you see-*
Over the loved ones who *walk with Christ Almighty.*

Holy, holy, holy-
Is my trust in God Almighty!!!

King Jesus, the heaven sent realm of hope, *is seated at our table of plenty*

<u>Barbara speaking to *King Jesus*</u>

Welcome into my home, *O sweet realm of hope and love.*
Thank you, *King Jesus, for sending the divine realm of hope that descended to us from heaven above.*

Oh how *grateful we are, dear Lord God-*
For you sent us *a taste of your heavenly love.*

FOR *HOLY AND TRUE-*
IS THE HOPE THAT *YOUR LOVED ONES HAVE IN YOU.*

HOLY, HOLY, HOLY-
IS MY HOPE IN CHRIST ALMIGHTY!!!

WHEN CHRIST, THE KING, *APPEARED TO ME*

<u>BARBARA SPEAKING</u>

MY ENTIRE *SOUL AND BODY-*
BOWED, AS *I WITNESSED THE HOLY PRESENCE OF CHRIST ALMIGHTY.*

HE APPEARED TO ME-
IN A *VISIBLE FORM THAT I DID SEE.*

I WEPT, YOU SEE-
BECAUSE *CHRIST, THE FOREVER-LIVING KING, CHOSE TO APPEAR TO LOWLY ME.*

HE APPEARED TO ME *ONE AFTERNOON-*
AS I FELL INTO A SPIRITUAL TRANCE, *WHILE PREPARING CLOTHES FOR THE LAUNDROMAT IN MY DAUGHTER'S BEDROOM.*

OH WHAT *AN HONOR, YOU SEE-*
TO BE VISITED BY *CHRIST* JESUS, *THE ALMIGHTY.*

HE APPEARED TO ME, ONCE, *AS A NEW BABY-*
HE WAS SURROUNDED BY LOVE AND DIVINE BEAUTY: HE WAS IN THE COMPANY OF *HIS EARTHLY FATHER JOSEPH, AND HIS EARTHLY MOTHER MARY.*

I BEHELD HIS GLORY-
AS I RECEIVED THE WORDS OF HIS HOLY STORY.

OH WHAT A DELIGHT-
TO BEHOLD THE KING'S HOLY PRESENCE WITHIN MY SIGHT.

WHEN CHRIST JESUS APPEARED TO ME-
I KNEW THAT I WOULD DO SOMETHING GOOD IN THE EYES OF GOD ALMIGHTY.

FOR HOLY, YOU SEE-
IS THE KING WHO APPEARED TO ME.

I BEHELD, YOU SEE-
THE HOLY KING WHO WAS SENT BY GOD, THE FATHER, TO RESCUE YOU AND ME.

HOLY, HOLY, HOLY-
IS THE HEAVENLY KING WHO APPEARED TO ME!!!

WHEN CHRIST, THE FOREVER-LIVING KING APPEARED TO ME.
HE SPOKE THE HOLY WORDS THAT SET ME FREE.

FOR HOLY AND REAL-
IS THE HEAVENLY KING WHO APPEARED TO ME, WHOM MY BLESSED SPIRIT COULD SEE AND FEEL.

FOR WITHIN HEAVEN'S OPEN GATES-
MY OBEDIENT SOUL SITS AND WAITS.

I CAN HEAR HIS HOLY COMMANDS AS HE SPEAKS TO ME; THEREFORE, I MOVE

BARBARA SPEAKING

I can hear *the king's holy commands-*
as he summons me with *the movements of his spiritual hands.*

I will now move, you see-
in the direction of *the holy god who calls out to me.*

Christ, the king, has spoken-
therefore, I will now leave my home and *mingle with his worthy children.*

I will *reveal, you see-*
everything that *he commands of me.*

I will go to those whom *the king loves, and does call.*
I will share his holy presence with his children, so that *their blessed souls will not fall.*

For *holy and true-*
are the king's words that *I share with blessed you.*

When Christ, the forever-living KING, speaks, *the worldly demons tremble and bow*

BARBARA SPEAKING

Speak. Speak. Speak, O holy Lord and God.
End the "unholy" presence of Satan's demons, *by the power of your holy love.*

RELEASE *YOUR WEAPON OF DIVINITY-*
AS THE DEMONS *TREMBLE IN THE PRESENCE OF GOD, THE ALMIGHTY.*

FOR *SATAN'S DEMONS, YOU SEE-*
WILL TREMBLE AND BOW *IN THE HOLY PRESENCE OF GOD ALMIGHTY; SWEET ETERNITY.*

FOR *HOLY AND REAL-*
IS THE KING'S VICTORIOUS PRESENCE THAT *SATAN'S DEFEATED DEMONS CAN TRULY FEEL.*

FOR WHEN *CHRIST JESUS SPEAKS, YOU SEE-*
SATAN'S DEMONS *TREMBLE WITH FEAR, IN THE PRESENCE OF GOD ALMIGHTY.*

HOLY, HOLY, HOLY-
IS THE SPIRITUAL WEAPONS OF GOD ALMIGHTY!!!

HIS HOLY WORDS OF LOVE *ARE VERY SHARP, YOU SEE-*
THEY ARE SENT OUT TO *DESTROY AND DEFEAT THE ENEMIES OF THE GREAT AND HOLY KING; CHRIST ALMIGHTY.*

THE HOLY KING'S WORDS *PENETRATE, YOU SEE-*
THE REALM OF EVIL AND DESTRUCTION THAT *TRIES TO HARM THE CHILDREN WHO BELONG TO GOD ALMIGHTY.*

HOLY, HOLY, HOLY-
ARE THE VICTORIOUS WORDS OF CHRIST, THE KING ALMIGHTY.

HOLY, HOLY, HOLY-
IS THE FOREVER-LIVING AND REIGNING GOD ALMIGHTY!!!

CHRIST, THE KING, SPEAKS TO ME DAILY, AND I LOVE HIS HOLY WORDS

BARBARA SPEAKING TO KING JESUS

SPEAK TO ME-
SPEAK TO ME, O GREAT WELL OF LOVE ALMIGHTY.

SPEAK TO ME IN MY LOVED ONES BLESSED PRESENCE-
SPEAK TO ME, KING JESUS, AS I PRAY TO YOU IN MY EARTHLY RESIDENCE.

FOR HOLY AND REAL-
ARE YOUR HEAVENLY WORDS THAT I CAN TRULY FEEL.

MY SOUL, MIND AND BODY-
BOW IN THE HOLY PRESENCE OF THE FOREVER-REIGNING CHRIST ALMIGHTY.

FOR I TRULY LOVE TO HEAR-
THE HOLY HEAVEN SENT WORDS THAT COME FROM THE MIGHTY KING WHO IS ALWAYS NEAR.

HOLY, HOLY, HOLY-
IS THE ETERNAL PRESENCE OF GOD ALMIGHTY.

WHEN CHRIST JESUS SPEAKS, I BOW, AS I LISTEN TO THE KING

BARBARA SPEAKING

WITH MY BLESSED HEAD BOWED LOW TOWARDS THE GROUND-
I LISTEN TO THE VOICE OF THE HOLY KING WHO IS ALWAYS AROUND.

When *he speaks, I do listen-*
For He reveals to me *Holy Words that He wants me to share with His beloved children.*

I listen to His Holy Words and Voice *every day.*
I listen, dear brothers and sisters, for *I long to hear what He has to say.*

For *His Holy Words of truth, you see-*
Give *everlasting life to you and me*

I sit very still-
As I receive the great and Holy *King's Heavenly Will.*

For *His Will, you see-*
Is to send *love and eternal life to you and me.*

Holy, holy, holy-
Is the Will of God Almighty!!!

When Christ, the KING, *walks in our midst*

<u>Barbara Speaking</u>

When *Christ* JESUS, *the King of Kings, walks-*
My blessed spirit talks.

For *Christ, the King, commands me-*
To speak *the Holy Words of God Almighty.*

When Christ, the King, *walks in our midst-*
My soul reveals to my loved ones and friends the truth, that *King* JESUS *does exist.*

For *holy and true-*
is the king who *walks in the midst of me and you.*

Christ *Jesus,* the forever-reigning king, *is in our midst right now: give him praise everyone*

<u>Barbara Speaking</u>

Christ *Jesus,* the forever reigning king, is *in our blessed midst, give him praise!*
The mighty heaven sent king *is in our midst during these pandemic days.*

Can you not see-
the spiritual presence of Christ almighty?

For *he walks in our midst-*
believe, dear brothers and sisters: *believe that his holy presence does exist.*

Believe! Believe! Believe!
Accept his holiness, as you receive.

For *king Jesus, you see-*
has *sent his holy words by me.*

Receive his divine light-
as he reveals his holy power and majesty within our blessed sight.

For *holy and real-*
is the presence of Christ, the king, that *the believing ones can truly see and feel.*

HE WALKS WITH US TODAY-
AS WE GO ABOUT OUR MERRY WAY.

DO NOT BE FOOLED, YOU SEE-
FOR KING JESUS DOES WALK IN THE MIDST OF YOU AND ME.

HOLY, HOLY, HOLY-
IS THE VISIBLE PRESENCE OF OUR FOREVER-RULING GOD:
CHRIST ALMIGHTY!!!

HOLY, HOLY, HOLY-
IS THE SPIRIT AND PRESENCE OF CHRIST JESUS, THE ALMIGHTY!!!

HE MOVES WITH ME THROUGHOUT EACH DAY

BARBARA SPEAKING TO KING JESUS

MOVE WITH ME, O GREAT AND HOLY KING OF KINGS.

SHARE WITH YOUR LOVED ONES ON EARTH, YOUR GOOD AND HOLY THINGS.

LET YOUR HOLY SPIRIT MOVE WITH ME TODAY-
AS I TEACH YOUR BLESSED CHILDREN HOW TO GIVE THANKS AND PRAY.

FOR OUR PRAYERS TO YOU-
SHOULD BE SINCERE AND TRUE.

FOR YOU, O HOLY KING AND GOD-
FOREVER SHARE WITH US, YOUR VERSION OF DIVINE LOVE.

HOLY, HOLY, HOLY-
IS THE LOVE OF GOD ALMIGHTY!!!

FOR YOU MOVE WITH YOUR LOVED ONES IN THE MIDST OF OUR SADNESS-
AND YOU BRIGHTEN OUR DAYS WITH THE PRESENCE OF YOUR GLORY AND HOLINESS.

GIVING THANKS TO KING JESUS EVERY DAY

<u>BARBARA SPEAKING</u>

I GIVE THANKS EVERY DAY-
TO KING JESUS, AS I BOW MY HUMBLED HEAD AND PRAY.

I GIVE THANKS FOR HIS REALM OF GOODNESS-
AS HE SHARES WITH HIS EARTHLY LOVED ONES, HIS DIVINITY AND GREATNESS.

MY MIND, BODY, AND SOUL APPRECIATE, YOU SEE-
EVERYTHING THAT KING JESUS HAS DONE FOR MY BELOVED FRIENDS AND FAMILY.

FOR HOLY, TRUE AND REAL-
ARE MY PRAYERS OF GRATITUDE THAT KING JESUS CAN TRULY FEEL.

CHRIST, THE FOREVER-LIVING KING, HAS SENT ME TO EXPOSE SATAN AND HIS DEMONS

BARBARA SPEAKING

I HAVE BEEN SENT, YOU SEE-
BY THE VICTORIOUS KING CALLED *CHRIST, THE ALMIGHTY.*

I HAVE BEEN SENT *TO EXPOSE, YOU SEE-*
THE DIRTY *WORKS OF SATAN; GOD'S ENEMY.*

FOR *HE DESIRES, YOU SEE-*
TO DESTROY *THE BLESSED SOULS OF YOU AND ME.*

HE DESIRES TO *DESTROY-*
EVERY GOD SEEKING GIRL AND BOY.

BE AWARE OF *SATAN'S "UNHOLY" PRESENCE-*
AS HE CREEPS IN *OUR EARTHLY HOMES AND RESIDENCE.*

BE AWARE OF *HIS DESTRUCTION-*
FOR HE HURTS *ALL OF THE KING'S GREAT CREATION.*

MY GREAT AND HOLY KING *JESUS,* HAS SENT ME *TO REVEAL* SATAN AND HIS FOLLOWERS

BARBARA SPEAKING

I HAVE BEEN SENT *TO LET YOU KNOW-*
THAT THE EVILS OF SATAN AND HIS DEFEATED ANGELS *FOLLOW GOD'S CHILDREN WHEREVER WE GO.*

HE FOLLOWS US *TO THE STORE-*
HE FOLLOWS US, *AS WE WALK THROUGH OUR CHURCHES OPEN DOOR.*

HE FOLLOWS US *TO OUR BEDS AT NIGHT-*
AS HE KEEPS US IN *HIS "UNHOLY" SIGHT.*

FOR HE IS *THE REALM OF EVIL AND DESTRUCTION-*
THAT TRIES VERY HARD TO *DESTROY ALL OF GOD'S WEAK AND VULNERABLE CHILDREN.*

BUT *KING JESUS, YOU SEE-*
HAS SENT *VICTORIOUS ME.*

FOR, *I DO FIGHT-*
THE REALM OF EVIL AND DESTRUCTION *EVERY DAY AND NIGHT.*

FOR *HOLY AND TRUE-*
IS THE KING WHO HAS SENT ME TO YOU.

BEHOLD! BEHOLD! BEHOLD! *BEHOLD THE MIGHTY KING WHO SITS AT MY TABLE OF PLENTY ON THANKSGIVING DAY*

<u>BARBARA SPEAKING</u>

BEHOLD CHRIST, THE KING-
WHO SITS AT MY TABLE OF PLENTY ON *THIS BLESSED THANKSGIVING.*

HE SITS, YOU SEE-
AT MY HEAVEN SENT *TABLE OF PLENTY.*

HE HAS GIVEN ME-
FOOD FROM THE HEAVENLY REALM AND HOME OF *THE KING ALMIGHTY.*

Oh how thankful I am today-
That the great and holy King led me to His life rewarding way.

For King Jesus has given me more-
Than what I had before.

He has provided for my daughter and me-
The gift of a beautiful free turkey.

Oh how grateful-
To belong to the Holy King who is eternal, good, and wonderful.

As I sit at my table of plenty-
I behold the Spirit of Christ Jesus, the Almighty.

For He dwells within-
The earthly home of Barbara, His messenger and friend.

Holy, Holy, Holy-
Is my heaven sent table of plenty.

For King Jesus, you see-
Has given plenty of food to my family, friends, and me.

Holy, Holy, Holy-
Is our thanksgiving to Christ Almighty!!!

I am truly grateful, for King Jesus, has graced me with His holy presence on this Thanksgiving Day (November 25, 2021)

BARBARA SPEAKING

IN *MY DEEPEST FORM OF THANKSGIVING*-
I BOW MY HEAD, AND *GIVE PRAISE, GLORY AND HONOR, TO CHRIST, THE KING.*

FOR AT *MY BLESSED TABLE*-
I AM GRACED WITH *THE PRESENCE OF THE ONLY GOD WHO IS ABLE.*

FOR *KING JESUS, YOU SEE*-
IS ABLE TO *FEED AND SAVE YOU AND ME.*

OH HOW GRAND IT IS-
TO BE *A MESSENGER AND DAUGHTER OF HIS.*

FOR *HIS HOLY PRESENCE*-
FILLS *MY EARTHLY RESIDENCE.*

HOLY, HOLY, HOLY-
IS THE MIGHTY KING WHO SHARES MY EARTHLY RESIDENCE WITH ME.

FOR HE MOVES *THROUGHOUT MY HOME,*
AND *I NEVER FEEL ALONE.*

HE GRACES ME WITH *HIS DIVINE PRESENCE*-
AS HIS HOLY SPIRIT *MOVES THROUGH MY BLESSED AND COMFORTABLE RESIDENCE.*

FOR *HOLY, YOU SEE*-
IS THE GOD AND KING WHO *DWELLS WITH BLESSED ME.*

HOLY, HOLY, HOLY-
IS OUR LIVING GOD AND KING; CHRIST ALMIGHTY!!!

WHEN CHRIST, THE HEAVEN SENT KING, SITS AT MY TABLE, I WILL JOIN HIM, AS I BOW

<u>*BARBARA SPEAKING TO KING JESUS*</u>

BE SEATED, LORD JESUS-
FOR IT IS AN HONOR TO SIT AT MY THANKSGIVING TABLE WITH THE HOLY GOD WHO SAVES US.

BE SEATED, MY HEAVEN SENT LOVE-
FOR I AM GRATEFUL TO BE IN THE PRESENCE OF THE HOLY KING WHO DESCENDS TO US FROM SWEET HEAVEN ABOVE.

FOR AS I SIT IN YOUR HOLY COMPANY-
I BOW MY SOUL AND SPIRIT IN THE PRESENCE OF MY GOD ALMIGHTY.

BE SEATED, DEAR ONE-
FOR IT IS A PRIVILEGE AND HONOR TO BE IN THE PRESENCE OF GOD, OUR HEAVENLY FATHER'S, ONLY BEGOTTEN SON.

BE SEATED, O GREAT AND MIGHTY KING-
FOR IT IS AN HONOR TO CELEBRATE WITH YOU, AS I OFFER YOU MY THANKSGIVING.

BE SEATED. BE SEATED. BE SEATED, MY BLESSED LORD AND GOD.
SIT WITH ME, KING JESUS, AT MY TABLE OF LOVE.

I WILL SERVE YOU ON THIS BLESSED THANKSGIVING DAY, *O GREAT AND HOLY KING JESUS*

<u>BARBARA SPEAKING TO KING JESUS</u>

I WILL GO OUT *ON THIS THANKSGIVING DAY-*
AND I WILL TELL YOUR LOVED ONES ABOUT *MY MINISTRY FOR YOU AND YOUR LIFE REWARDING HOLY WAY.*

ON THIS THANKSGIVING MORNING, *I WILL GO WHEREVER YOU SEND ME-*
SO THAT I MAY SHOW YOUR LOVED ONES *THE HOLY WORDS THAT YOU HAVE DICTATED TO ME.*

I WILL *FOLLOW YOUR LEAD, O HOLY GOD-*
AS YOU *LEAD ME TO THOSE WHOM YOU LOVE.*

I WILL SPEAK-
TO THOSE WHOM *YOUR BLESSED HOLY SPIRIT DOES SEEK.*

I WILL SHARE *THE WORDS THAT YOU SAY-*
ON THIS *BLESSED THANKSGIVING DAY.*

WHEN CHRIST, THE FOREVER-LIVING KING, *EATS MY PREPARED MEAL*

<u>BARBARA SPEAKING</u>

I HAVE PREPARED *A HOMEMADE MEAL, YOU SEE-*
FOR OUR *FOREVER-LIVING GOD ALMIGHTY.*

HE IS VERY PLEASED, YOU SEE-
FOR MY PREPARED MEAL WAS *BAPTIZED AND SANCTIFIED BY HOLY HE.*

OH HOW EXCITING-
TO HAVE PREPARED AN ACCEPTABLE MEAL FOR GOD ALMIGHTY, THE HEAVEN SENT KING!

FOR *KING JESUS,* YOU SEE-
SHARED THE PREPARED MEAL THAT WAS *MADE BY ME.*

HE SHARED IT-
BY *THE POWER OF HIS HOLY SPIRIT.*

HE SHARED *THE MEAL,* YOU SEE-
WITH THOSE WHO ARE *CALLED AND CHOSEN BY HOLY HE.*

AND HE SHARED ME *WITH HIS EARTHLY LOVED ONES-*
YES! HE SHARED ME WITH *HIS BELOVED DAUGHTERS AND SONS.*

FOR HE SENDS ME WITH *HIS WORDS THAT COME FROM SWEET HEAVEN ABOVE.*
SO THAT I MAY SHARE THEM WITH *THOSE WHOM HE DOES LOVE.*

HOLY, HOLY, HOLY-
IS THE MEAL THAT I HAVE PREPARED FOR CHRIST ALMIGHTY!!!

AND THE SPIRIT OF THE EVERLASTING KING DANCES WITH ME

BARBARA SPEAKING

THROUGHOUT EACH DAY-
AS I MOVE WITHIN THE KING'S LIFE SAVING WAY:

MY SPIRIT DANCES, YOU SEE-
WITH THE FOREVER-LIVING KING CALLED CHRIST ALMIGHTY.

HIS HOLY SPIRIT MOVES AND DANCES IN MY BLESSED MIDST-
AS I BOW IN THE PRESENCE OF THE KING WHO DOES EXIST.

MY SPIRIT GLIDES-
FOR THE KING RELEASES A LOVE THAT HE NEVER HIDES.

FOR HIS LOVE IS REAL-
IT IS A LOVE THAT THE REALM OF DARKNESS CANNOT DESTROY OR STEAL.

I MOVE WITH THE BEATS THAT WERE RELEASED FROM THE THRONE OF MY MIGHTY KING AND GOD.
I MOVE WITH THE SOUND OF HIS RELEASED REALM OF DIVINE MERCY AND LOVE.

I MOVE EACH AND EVERY DAY-
IN THE MIDST OF HIS HEAVEN SENT HOLY WAY.

HOLY, HOLY, HOLY-
ARE THE DANCES OF THE GREAT AND HOLY KING ALMIGHTY!!!

DID YOU HEAR THE HOLY VOICE OF THE KING TODAY?

BARBARA SPEAKING

Dear Brother: Dear Sister-
Dear you hear the Holy voice of God, our King and Father?

Did you hear Him calling out to you?
Did you listen to the Voice that is Holy, Eternal and True?

For King Jesus, you see-
Calls out to you and me.

Did you hear our Blessed Savior Speak-
As He called out to those whom His blessed Spirit did seek?

Did you hear His Holy Voice today-
As He led you to His life saving Holy way?

When Christ, The King, Beckons Me

BARBARA SPEAKING

When the Great and Holy God and King beckons me-
I immediately head in the direction of the Voice and Spirit of Christ Almighty.

I follow, you see-
The Holy Spirit that beckons me.

I will follow Christ, The King-
To a world that shares His good news and thing.

FOR *HOLY AND REAL-*
IS THE BLESSED SPIRIT OF THE KING THAT *I CAN FEEL.*

HOLY, HOLY, HOLY-
IS THE BECKONING HAND OF GOD ALMIGHTY!!!

I WILL ENTER *THE KING'S HOLY WORLD*

<u>BARBARA SPEAKING</u>

IT IS A SMALL PLACE *WITHIN THE REALM OF REALITY AND EXISTENCE.*
IT IS A PLACE THAT IS *RULED AND GOVERNED BY GOD'S HOLY PRESENCE.*

IT IS A PLACE THAT IS *VERY NEAR, YOU SEE-*
FOR IT IS *THE WORLD THAT IS RULED BY THE ALMIGHTY.*

I WILL ENTER, YOU SEE-
THE HOLY WORLD THAT *CALLS OUT TO BLESSED ME.*

FOR *WITHIN THAT SMALL WORLD, YOU SEE-*
IS *THE POWERFUL THRONE OF CHRIST ALMIGHTY.*

HOLY, HOLY, HOLY-
IS THE PRIVATE WORLD OF GOD ALMIGHTY!!!

THERE IS *A WORLD OF EVIL THAT EXISTS*

<u>BARBARA SPEAKING</u>

IN OUR MIDST-
THERE IS *A WORLD OF EVIL THAT DOES EXIST.*

THIS WORLD OF EVIL *ROAMS IN THE MIDST OF US-*
AND IS INHABITED BY BEINGS THAT *DO NOT HONOR OR RESPECT KING JESUS.*

THIS WORLD OF EVIL, *YOU SEE-*
DOESN'T FEAR OR *HONOR CHRIST ALMIGHTY.*

THIS WICKED WORLD, *YOU SEE-*
HAS CAPTURED AND *DECEIVED MANY.*

FOR *THE INHABITANTS OF THIS WORLD-*
HAS FOOLED AND CAPTURED *THE UNSUSPECTING BOY AND GIRL.*

THIS WORLD OF EVIL, YOU KNOW-
FOLLOWS THE DECEIVED ONES *WHEREVER THEY GO.*

THE INHABITANTS OF *THIS EVIL PLACE-*
DO NOT BOW DOWN IN THE PRESENCE OF *KING JESUS' HOLY FACE.*

FOR *SATAN, THE DECEPTIVE ONE-*
HAS CAPTURED *THE VULNERABLE AND WEAK DAUGHTER AND SON.*

BEING WITH CHRIST, THE *KING, ON THIS BLESSED THANKSGIVING DAY (NOVEMBER 25, 2021)*

<u>BARBARA SPEAKING</u>

SITTING IN MY MIDST-
IS *THE HEAVENLY KING WHO DOES EXIST.*

FOR ON THIS *THANKSGIVING DAY*-
KING *JESUS* CAME TO ME, *AS MY SPIRIT AND SOUL DID PRAY.*

THE *KING AND I REJOICED AS ONE*-
AS I SHARED MY THANKSGIVING MEAL WITH *GOD, THE FATHER'S, ONLY BEGOTTEN SON.*

OH WHAT *A DIVINE PLEASURE*-
FOR THE HOLY PRESENCE OF KING *JESUS* SITTING AT MY TABLE OF PLENTY, *I WILL FOREVER TREASURE.*

FOR *HOLY AND TRUE*-
IS THE PRESENCE OF *THE MIGHTY KING WHO LOVES ME AND YOU.*

HOLY, HOLY, HOLY-
IS THE PRESENCE OF THE CHRIST ALMIGHTY.

COME, DEAR SISTERS AND BROTHERS, *AND LOOK UPON CHRIST JESUS, YOUR SOVEREIGN GOD AND KING*

<u>BARBARA SPEAKING</u>

BEHOLD HIM, DEAR SISTER! BEHOLD HIM, DEAR BROTHER!
COME, AND LOOK UPON *THE HEAVEN SENT GIFT FROM GOD, OUR FATHER!*

COME OUT TODAY-
AND LISTEN TO WHAT *OUR HEAVEN SENT GIFT HAS TO SAY.*

FOR *KING JESUS, YOU SEE*-
IS THE HEAVEN SENT GIFT THAT WAS *GIVEN TO YOU AND ME.*

REJOICE! REJOICE! REJOICE!
COME, ALL YOU BLESSED ONES, AND HEAR KING JESUS' HOLY VOICE!

FOR HE SPEAKS TO US TODAY-
HE SPEAKS TO ALL WHO BOW IN HIS HOLY PRESENCE AS THEY PRAY.

BEHOLD THE SOVEREIGN ONE!
BEHOLD CHRIST JESUS, FOR HE IS GOD, THE FATHER'S, ONLY BEGOTTEN SON!

BEHOLD THE SAVIOR OF THE WORLD!
BEHOLD THE CREATOR AND ORIGIN OF EVERY BLESSED BOY AND GIRL!

LOOK UPON OUR HEAVEN SENT GIFT FROM ABOVE!
LOOK UPON KING JESUS, THE ORIGIN OF DIVINE LOVE!

FOR HOLY AND TRUE-
IS THE HEAVEN SENT GIFT FROM GOD, THE FATHER, WHO DESCENDED TO ME AND YOU.

HOLY, HOLY, HOLY-
IS THE HEAVEN SENT GIFT CALLED CHRIST JESUS; THE EVERLASTING KING ALMIGHTY!!!

CHRIST *JESUS, THE ROYAL ONE*

BARBARA SPEAKING

CHRIST JESUS, THE HOLY ROYAL ONE-
HAS ENTERED THE REALM OF *HIS WORTHY DAUGHTER AND SON.*

HE HAS ENTERED WITH *DIVINE MAJESTY AND STYLE.*
FOR HE PLANS ON *STAYING WITH HIS EARTHLY LOVED ONES FOR A WHILE.*

HE IS THE *HEAVEN SENT ROYAL ONE, YOU SEE-*
AND HIS DIVINE MISSION IS TO *DWELL WITH YOU AND ME.*

FOR *GOD, OUR HEAVENLY FATHER, YOU SEE-*
SENT *CHRIST, THE ROYAL KING, TO YOU AND ME.*

FOR *HOLY AND TRUE-*
IS THE GOD AND FATHER WHO *REALLY LOVES ME AND YOU.*

HOLY, HOLY, HOLY-
IS THE ROYAL HEAVEN SENT ONE CALLED CHRIST ALMIGHTY!!!

I AM NEVER ALONE, FOR *CHRIST JESUS, THE ROYAL KING, SITS AT MY SIDE THROUGHOUT EVERY DAY*

BARBARA SPEAKING

I AM NEVER ALONE, YOU SEE-
FOR CHRIST, THE FOREVER-LIVING KING, IS ALWAYS SITTING RIGHT NEXT TO ME.

HE IS WITH ME AS I MOVE THROUGHOUT THE DAY.
HE IS ALSO WITH ME WHEN MY BLESSED SPIRIT KNEELS AND PRAY.

FOR HOLY IS THE GOD, YOU SEE-
WHO WATCHES OVER SENT AND OBEDIENT ME.

FOR KING JESUS, YOU SEE-
SENT OBEDIENT AND FAITHFUL ME.

HOLY, HOLY, HOLY-
IS THE VISIBLE PRESENCE OF CHRIST JESUS, THE HEAVEN SENT KING ALMIGHTY!!!

DIVINE ROYALTY HAS STEPPED INTO OUR PHYSICAL WORLD

BARBARA SPEAKING

HE HAS ENTERED OUR WORLD-
YES! CHRIST JESUS, WHO IS DIVINE RULER AND KING OVER EVERY SAVED BOY AND GIRL.

FOR CHRIST, THE DIVINE RULER, YOU SEE-
HAS STEPPED INTO THE PHYSICAL WORLD THAT SHELTERS YOU AND ME.

FOR *CHRIST, THE ROYAL ONE-*
IS *GOD, THE FATHER'S, ONLY BEGOTTEN DIVINE SON.*

FOR *HOLY AND TRUE-*
IS *THE ROYAL KING WHO RULES OVER ME AND YOU.*

HOLY, HOLY, HOLY-
ARE *THE SUBJECTS OF THE KING ALMIGHTY!!!*

FOR *HIS MAJESTY-*
SHINES *IN THE MIDST OF YOU AND ME.*

I BEHELD *THE MAJESTIC KING ALMIGHTY-*
AS *HE STEPPED INTO THE WORLD THAT SHELTERS YOU AND ME.*

FOR *HOLY AND TRUE-*
IS *THE KING WHO WATCHES OVER ME AND YOU.*

BEHOLD *THE KING*

<u>BARBARA SPEAKING</u>

BEHOLD THE MIGHTY ONE!
BEHOLD *GOD, THE FATHER'S, VICTORIOUS SON!*

BEHOLD *CHRIST, THE FOREVER-REIGNING KING!*
BEHOLD THE ETERNAL SON WHO *BRINGS A GOOD AND HOLY THING.*

FOR *KING JESUS, YOU SEE*-
BRINGS *THE GOOD NEWS THAT WILL SAVE YOU AND ME.*

HE BRINGS WITH HIM *THE GIFT OF SALVATION*-
WHICH IS OFFERED TO *THOSE FROM EVERY NATION.*

DEAR *BROTHERS AND SISTERS OF MINE*-
CLING TO THE KING'S GOOD NEWS THAT *LAST THROUGHOUT THE REALM OF UNSEEN TIME.*

FOR *HOLY AND TRUE*-
IS THE GOOD THING (NEWS) THE HE SHARES WITH ME AND YOU.

I WILL HOLD ON TIGHT TO THE KING'S ROBE THAT IS *WITHIN MY BLESSED SIGHT*

BARBARA SPEAKING

I WILL HOLD ON TIGHT, YOU SEE-
TO THE BOTTOM OF *THE KING'S ROYAL ROBE AS HE LEADS ME.*

FOR *HE LEADS ME, YOU SEE-*
TO THE HEAVENLY HOME OF *GOD, THE FATHER, ALMIGHTY.*

FOR, AT THE BOTTOM OF *THE KING'S ROYAL ROBE, YOU SEE-*
IS A PLACE THAT CALLS OUT TO ME.

FOR THE KING'S ROBE IS *STRONG AND MIGHTY-*
IT IS THE ROYAL ROBE THAT *LEADS TRUSTING ME.*

FOR *THE DIVINE STRENGTH THAT HOLDS ME-*
COMES FROM *THE ROYAL ROBE THAT IS WORN BY THE HEAVEN SENT KING ALMIGHTY.*

HOLY, HOLY, HOLY-
IS THE ROYAL ROBE OF CHRIST ALMIGHTY!!!

THE ROYAL ROBE THAT *COMFORTS ME EVERY DAY*

BARBARA SPEAKING

COMFORT MY WEARY SOUL THROUGHOUT EACH DAY, *O BLESSED ROBE OF CHRIST JESUS.*
RELEASE *THE COMFORT AND JOY THAT IS AVAILABLE TO ALL OF US.*

RELEASE *YOUR REALM OF UNENDING LOVE-*
AS YOUR BELIEVING LOVED ONES GIVE PRAISE, GLORY AND HONOR, *TO THE MIGHTY KING WHO DESCENDED TO US FROM SWEET HEAVEN ABOVE.*

I SALUTE THE GREAT AND HOLY ROYAL KING, *AS HE SITS ON HIS MIGHTY THRONE ABOVE.*
I REJOICE IN THE COMFORT OF THE KING'S ROYAL ROBE *AS IT RELEASES BLESSINGS AND DIVINE LOVE.*

FOR *HOLY, YOU SEE-*
IS THE KING'S ROYAL ROBE THAT *GIVES COMFORT TO BLESSED ME.*

HOLY, HOLY, HOLY-
IS THE COMFORT GIVING ROBE OF CHRIST ALMIGHTY!!!

AS MY SPIRIT HOLDS ON TO *THE KING'S ROYAL ROBE OF DIVINE LOVE*

BARBARA SPEAKING

MY BLESSED SPIRIT HOLDS ON TO *THE ROYAL ROBE OF KING JESUS, THE HOLY ONE.*
MY MIND CLINGS TO *THE GIFT OF GOD, THE FATHER'S, ONLY BEGOTTEN SON.*

AS MY BLESSED SPIRIT *CLINGS TO THE KING'S HOLY ROYAL ROBE OF LOVE-*

MY BODY AND SOUL *BOW IN THE PRESENCE OF THE SAVIOR AND KING WHO DESCENDED FROM HEAVEN ABOVE.*

FOR *KING JESUS' HOLY ROBE, YOU SEE-*
HAS BEEN PLACED UPON *THE SPIRIT OF THE MESSENGER (BARBARA) AND DAUGHTER OF GOD ALMIGHTY.*

FOR *MY SPIRIT DESIRED, YOU SEE-*
TO FEEL THE HOLY ROBE THAT *BELONGS TO CHRIST JESUS, THE ROYAL KING ALMIGHTY.*

HOLY, HOLY, HOLY-
IS THE ROYAL ROBE OF CHRIST ALMIGHTY!!!

AS MY MIND, BODY AND SOUL *SNUGGLE WITHIN THE ROYAL ROBE OF CHRIST, THE FOREVER REIGNING KING*

BARBARA SPEAKING

OH *THE COMFORT AND WARMTH THAT I RECEIVE-*
FOR I SNUGGLE WITHIN *THE ROYAL ROBE THAT BELONGS TO THE SACRED GOD AND KING, IN WHOM I TRULY BELIEVE.*

FOR *I TRULY BELIEVE IN-*
THE HOLY GOD AND KING WHO *DWELLS WITHIN.*

FOR *WITHIN ME-*
DWELLS *THE ROYAL HOLY SPIRIT OF THE FOREVER-REIGNING KING ALMIGHTY.*

FOR *CHRIST JESUS, YOU SEE-*
IS THE ROYAL KING WHO *REIGNS AND RULES OVER BELIEVING AND OBEDIENT ME.*

HOLY, HOLY, HOLY-
IS THE ROYAL ROBE OF CHRIST ALMIGHTY!!!

MY BLESSED SPIRIT *BOWS IN THE HOLY PRESENCE OF CHRIST, THE* KING, *AND HIS ROYAL ROBE*

BARBARA SPEAKING

MY BLESSED SPIRIT *BOWS, YOU SEE-*
AS I ENTER THE HOLY PRESENCE OF *CHRIST, THE KING OF DIVINE ROYALTY.*

MY *IGNITED SPIRIT REJOICES-*
AS I JOIN *THE KING'S HEAVENLY CHOIRS HOLY VOICES.*

FOR IN THE PRESENCE OF *THE ROYAL ROBE, YOU SEE-*
I BOW AND GIVE HOMAGE TO *THE GREAT AND HOLY KING ALMIGHTY.*

FOR *KING* JESUS, *YOU SEE-*
WEARS THE ROYAL ROBE THAT *OFFERS GREAT JOY AND COMFORT TO BLESSED ME.*

HOLY, HOLY, HOLY-
IS THE ROYAL ROBE THAT IS WORN BY CHRIST JESUS, THE ETERNAL KING ALMIGHTY!!!

I CAN HEAR THE KING'S HOLY ANGELS *AS I GIVE HIM PRAISE*

BARBARA SPEAKING

I CAN HEAR. I CAN HEAR. I CAN HEAR-
I CAN HEAR THE SOUND OF THE KING'S HOLY ANGELS, FOR *THEY ARE VERY NEAR.*

OH WHAT A GLORIOUS SOUND-
THAT THROUGHOUT THE DAY, *MY SOUL DOES SURROUND.*

FOR THE *KING'S ANGELS, YOU SEE-*
SURROUND *THE BLESSED SOUL THAT BELONGS TO ME.*

I CAN HEAR THEIR VOICES-
AS *MY SOUL REJOICES.*

FOR THEY DO *SING WITH GLADNESS-*
AS *CHRIST, THE KING, REVEALS HIS HOLINESS.*

FOR *THE HOLINESS OF CHRIST, THE HEAVENLY KING, YOU SEE-*
MOVES AND WALKS WITH BLESSED ME.

FOR *HE GRANTS, YOU SEE-*
THE PRESENCE OF HIS HOLY ANGELS TO *WALK AND SING WITH ME.*

OH HOW EXCITING IT IS-
TO BE A WITNESS TO *THE VISIBILITY OF THE ANGELS THAT ARE HIS.*

FOR *CHRIST JESUS' ANGELS, YOU SEE-*
LOVES TO *SING AND DANCE WITH ME.*

HOLY, HOLY, HOLY-
ARE THE DANCING ANGELS OF CHRIST ALMIGHTY!!!

PRAISE! PRAISE! PRAISE!
LET US LIFT UP OUR SONGS AND DANCE IN THE HOLY PRESENCE OF KING JESUS, DURING THESE PANDEMIC DAYS!!!

HALLELUJAH! HALLELUJAH! HALLELUJAH-
TO THE *REJOICING SON OF GOD, OUR FATHER, JEHOVAH!!!*

FOR *HOLY AND TRUE-*
IS THE KING WHO REJOICES WITH ME AND YOU.

THEY, THE KINGS HOLY ANGELS, *SURROUND HIS HOLY THRONE ON HIGH*

<u>BARBARA SPEAKING</u>

I CAN SEE! I CAN SEE!
I CAN SEE THE HOLY ANGELS *AS THEY SURROUND THE THRONE OF THE GREAT AND HOLY KING ALMIGHTY!!!*

I CAN HEAR THEIR CONTINUOUS PRAISE-
AS THEY WITNESS MY SERVITUDE AND MINISTRY DURING THESE PANDEMIC DAYS.

FOR *HOLY AND REAL-*
ARE THE ANGELS PRAISES THAT *THE KING AND I CAN TRULY SEE AND FEEL.*

FOR *KING JESUS, YOU SEE-*
HAS JOINED THE PRAISES, *AS THEY REACHED THE MIGHTY THRONE OF GOD, THE FATHER; SWEET ETERNITY.*

FOR *WITHIN OUR MIDST-*
SWEET ETERNITY'S (GOD, THE FATHER) HOLY PRESENCE DOES EXIST.

HOLY, HOLY, HOLY-
IS THE EXISTING PRESENCE OF ALMIGHTY GOD; SWEET ETERNITY!!!

AS MY BLESSED SPIRIT SITS ON THE MIGHTY HEAVENLY THRONE OF KING JESUS

<u>BARBARA SPEAKING</u>

MY BLESSED SPIRIT BOWS, YOU SEE-
FOR IT IS IN THE HOLY PRESENCE OF THE KING ALMIGHTY.

MY SPIRIT BOWS IN THE PRESENCE OF CHRIST, THE KING-
FOR HE HAS GRACED AND HONORED ME WITH A WONDERFUL THING.

HE HAS GRACED ME WITH A GIFT, YOU SEE-
A GIFT THAT WAS APPROVED BY GOD, THE FATHER, ALMIGHTY.

FOR UPON HIS MIGHTY THRONE OF LOVE-
MY BLESSED SPIRIT WAS GRANTED THE PRIVILEGE AND HONOR, TO SIT ON THE THRONE THAT SITS IN SWEET HEAVEN ABOVE.

FOR JEHOVAH GOD, OUR FATHER, YOU SEE-
APPROVES OF OBEDIENT AND WORTHY ME.

HE HAS PERMITTED ME-
TO SHARE THE HOLY THRONE OF CHRIST ALMIGHTY.

FOR HOLY AND TRUE-
IS THE GOD AND FATHER WHO REALLY LOVES ME AND YOU.

HOLY, HOLY, HOLY-
IS OUR GOD AND FATHER, JEHOVAH ALMIGHTY!!!

THE MIGHTY THRONE OF CHRIST, THE FOREVER-REIGNING KING

BARBARA SPEAKING

IT HAS DESCENDED TO US FROM SWEET HEAVEN ABOVE-
AND NOW, I WILL REJOICE IN THE PRESENCE OF KING JESUS' THRONE OF LOVE.

FOR HIS MIGHTY THRONE, YOU SEE-
HOLDS THE HOLY SPIRIT AND PRESENCE OF CHRIST ALMIGHTY.

THE KING'S THRONE OF LOVE-
SENDS DOWN HIS DIVINE MESSAGES FROM HEAVEN ABOVE.

FOR HOLY AND TRUE-
IS THE THRONE THAT SITS IN THE SPIRITUAL PRESENCE OF ME AND YOU.

HOLY, HOLY, HOLY-
IS THE THRONE OF CHRIST JESUS, THE ROYAL KING ALMIGHTY!!!

FOR HE SITS, YOU SEE-
ON THE THRONE THAT WILL EXIST THROUGHOUT ETERNITY.

CHRIST JESUS: MY KING, MY GOD; AND MY SAVIOR

BARBARA SPEAKING

HE IS REAL!
FOR HIS DIVINITY, MY SPIRIT, BODY AND SOUL, CAN TRULY FEEL!

HE IS MY LORD AND GOD-
HE IS THE KING AND SAVIOR WHO *DESCENDED TO US FROM SWEET HEAVEN ABOVE.*

HE IS THE SANCTIFIER-
WHO HAS MADE PURE AND HOLY, *ME, HIS SENT MESSENGER AND OBEDIENT DAUGHTER.*

FOR *CHRIST, THE KING, YOU SEE-*
HAS *PURIFIED SENT AND OBEDIENT ME.*

HE PURIFIED ME OF *THE SINS OF MY PAST-*
AND HAS GIVEN ME *A DIVINE ASSIGNMENT THAT WILL FOREVER LAST.*

FOR *HE HAS SENT ME-*
TO SPEAK TO *THE CALLED AND CHOSEN ONES OF CHRIST ALMIGHTY.*

FOR *MY DIVINE ASSIGNMENT, YOU SEE-*
WILL HELP *THE CAPTIVE ONES BECOME FREE.*

FOR *KING JESUS, YOU SEE-*
SENT BLESSED ME.

HOLY, HOLY, HOLY-
ARE THE HEAVENLY ASSIGNMENTS OF GOD ALMIGHTY!!!

I WILL NOT MOVE UNTIL *CHRIST, THE FOREVER-LIVING KING,* TELLS ME TO

BARBARA SPEAKING

I WILL SIT-
AND *I WILL NOT QUIT.*

I WILL NOT MOVE AND INCH, YOU SEE-
UNTIL *CHRIST, THE KING, BECKONS ME.*

I WILL SIT VERY STILL-
AS *I SENSE HIS HOLY WILL.*

FOR *I DO KNOW, YOU SEE-*
THE HOLY SPIRIT AND VOICE OF *THE ETERNAL KING, WHO SPEAKS DAILY TO LISTENING ME.*

FOR *HIS HOLY VOICE, YOU SEE-*
LEADS AND COMMANDS OBEDIENT ME.

I WILL SIT QUIETLY-
AS I LISTEN FOR *THE HOLY PRESENCE OF MY KING AND GOD ALMIGHTY.*

FOR *HOLY AND TRUE-*
IS *THE SPIRIT OF THE KING WHO SENDS ME TO YOU.*

HOLY, HOLY, HOLY-
IS THE FOREVER-LIVING KING; CHRIST ALMIGHTY!!!

WHEN CHRIST, THE KING, CAME TO ME THE NEXT MORNING

BARBARA SPEAKING

MY ARMS AND BLESSED SPIRIT *ARE OPEN WIDE-*
AS I RELEASE THE INNER LOVE THAT *MY MIND, BODY AND SOUL REFUSE TO HIDE.*

FOR *I WAS GREETED THE NEXT MORNING-*
BY *THE HOLY SPIRIT AND PRESENCE OF GOD, MY KING.*

HIS HOLY SPIRIT AND PRESENCE *DID AWAKEN-*
HIS DAUGHTER; YES, *HIS SENT MESSENGER, AND ONE OF HIS CHOSEN.*

FOR, *THE NEXT MORNING-*
I WAS GREETED BY *THE GIFT OF CHRIST JESUS; HEAVEN'S SENT KING.*

FOR *KING JESUS, YOU SEE-*
CAME TO *COMFORT AND WALK WITH ME.*

FOR *HE CAME THE NEXT MORNING, YOU SEE-*
TO *TEACH, LOVE AND GUIDE BLESSED ME.*

HE CAME *WITHOUT A VERBAL SOUND-*
BUT I KNEW THAT *HIS GLORIOUS SPIRIT WAS AROUND.*

FOR *I FELT THE WARMTH, YOU SEE-*
THAT COMES FROM *THE HOLY SPIRIT OF GOD ALMIGHTY.*

HOLY, HOLY, HOLY-
IS THE INVISIBLE PRESENCE OF CHRIST *JESUS, THE KING ALMIGHTY!!!*

When Christ, the KING, speaks, *as he places his royal crown upon his head*

<u>Barbar Speaking</u>

In the Holy King's Presence, *I can see-*
The Royal Crown of Christ Almighty.

In His Holy Presence-
I salute the Mighty King *as He joins me in my earthly residence.*

I will listen to Him, for *He is about to speak.*
He is about to tell me about *the souls of those whom His Holy Spirit will seek.*

As He places His Holy Crown upon His Royal Head, you see-
I bow in the presence of *Divine Majesty.*

For *King* JESUS, *you see-*
Is about to *speak to me.*

I will listen to His every words, you see-
For His words are *pure and holy.*

With His Holy Crown *upon His Royal Head of Love-*
I bow down in the presence of *the King who descended to us from Heaven above.*

Holy, Holy, Holy-
Is Christ, the King, Almighty!!!

MY BLESSED SPIRIT AND SOUL *BOW IN THE PRESENCE OF THE HOLY CROWN OF KING JESUS*

BARBARA SPEAKING

BOW! BOW! BOW! BOW, O BLESSED SPIRIT OF MINE!
GIVE GLORY AND HONOR TO *CHRIST JESUS' ROYAL CROWN DURING THIS PANDEMIC PERIOD OF TIME.*

FOR *CHRIST, THE HOLY KING OF KINGS-*
BRINGS TO US *GOOD TIDINGS.*

FOR *THE CROWN THAT HE WEARS-*
REMOVES THE BELIEVING ONES *REALM OF FEARS.*

FOR *CHRIST JESUS' HOLY CROWN TODAY-*
BRINGS PEACE AND JOY TO US WHENEVER WE PRAY.

FOR *HOLY AND TRUE-*
IS THE HEAVENLY KING WHO *SEES HIS TRUSTING SUBJECTS THROUGH.*

HOLY, HOLY, HOLY-
IS THE ROYAL CROWN OF CHRIST ALMIGHTY!!!

THE KING'S ROYAL CROWN AND ME

BARBARA SPEAKING

IN THE *HOLY PRESENCE OF CHRIST JESUS' ROYAL CROWN-*
I BOW IN THE MIDST OF *HIS ANGELS HOLY SOUND.*

FOR THEIR *HOLY AND JOYOUS SOUND-*
LET ME KNOW THAT *KING JESUS' HOLY SPIRIT IS ALWAYS AROUND.*

MY BLESSED *MIND, SOUL AND BODY-*
JOIN *THE ANGELS OF CHRIST ALMIGHTY.*

HOLY, HOLY, HOLY-
IS THE *ROYAL CROWN OF GOD ALMIGHTY!!!*

FOR *IN OUR BLESSED MIDST-*
WE SALUTE *THE HEAVENLY GOD AND KING WHO DOES EXIST.*

HOLY, HOLY, HOLY-
IS THE *ROYAL CROWN OF CHRIST ALMIGHTY!!!*

THE HOLY CROWN THAT *TRAVELED TO OUR REALM OF EXISTENCE TODAY*

BARBARA SPEAKING

THE HOLY AND ROYAL CROWN OF KING JESUS-
MOVES AND RESIDES *IN THE MIDST OF THE RIGHTEOUS.*

FOR I AM BLESSED *TO FEEL AND SEE-*
THE HEAVEN SENT *ROYAL CROWN OF CHRIST ALMIGHTY.*

I SALUTE *THE HOLY CROWN OF KING JESUS-*
THAT *EXISTS IN THE MIDST OF ALL OF US.*

FOR *HOLY AND TRUE-*
IS THE KING'S CROWN THAT IS *VISIBLE TO ME AND YOU.*

HOLY, HOLY, HOLY-
IS THE ROYAL HEAVENLY CROWN OF GOD ALMIGHTY!!!

I CAN SEE *THE LUMINOUS CROWN OF CHRIST JESUS, THE HEAVEN SENT KING*

BARBARA SPEAKING

I CAN SEE! I CAN SEE! I CAN REALLY SEE-
THE LUMINOUS CROWN OF GOD ALMIGHTY!!!

I CAN SEE IT-
BY *THE DIVINE POWER OF KING JESUS' HOLY SPIRIT!*

FOR *HIS LIGHT OF LOVE-*
ILLUMINATES THE ROYAL CROWN OF *THE KING THAT DESCENDED TO US FROM SWEET HEAVEN ABOVE.*

HOLY, HOLY, HOLY-
IS THE LUMINOUS CROWN OF *THE KING ALMIGHTY!!!*

IN THE MIDDLE OF THE NIGHT, *I CAN SEE THE VISIBILITY OF THE KING'S CROWN*

BARBARA SPEAKING

*THROUGHOUT THE BLESSED NIGHT-
KING JESUS' ROYAL CROWN IS WITHIN MY SPIRITUAL SIGHT.*

*THROUGHOUT THE BLESSED DAY-
THE KING'S ROYAL CROWN LEADS ME TO THE KING'S HOLY LIFE REWARDING WAY.*

FOR *KING JESUS' HOLY CROWN, YOU SEE-
ILLUMINATES EVERYTHING AROUND BLESSED ME.*

YES! *HIS CROWN OF DIVINE LIGHT-*
GIVES MY SOUL PEACE AND COMFORT *THROUGHOUT THE DARKEST NIGHT.*

*HOLY, HOLY, HOLY-
IS THE LUMINOUS CROWN OF CHRIST ALMIGHTY!!!*

WHEN CHRIST, THE FOREVER-LIVING KING, *WAKES ME THE NEXT MORNING*

BARBARA SPEAKING

MY BLESSED *EYES HAVE OPENED AGAIN-
AND NOW, I AM IN THE HOLY PRESENCE OF MY ETERNAL HEAVENLY FRIEND.*

HE HAS OPENED MY EYES *ON THIS BLESSED DAY-
SO THAT I MAY SPEAK OF HIS LIFE SAVING HOLY WAY.*

He opened my eyes this God ordered morning-
and now, my blessed soul rejoices in the presence of my life saving King.

For Holy and True-
is the King who brings me through.

For, as the next day approaches for me-
I can feel the Holy Spirit of God almighty.

For His Holy Spirit-
speaks to me, so that I may hear it.

I can hear-
the spoken words of the Holy One who is very near.

For Holy and Real-
is the presence of Christ, the King, that I can truly feel.

Holy, Holy, Holy-
is the presence of Christ almighty!!!

Divine mysteries and secrets that descended to me from sweet Heaven above

<u>Barbara speaking</u>

Through the years, the Lord God has revealed some of heaven's valuable mysteries and secrets to me. I was graced and privilege to behold some of the wonders of Christ Jesus, the King almighty.

Christ, the forever-living King, revealed to me-
the many things that would help the children of God Almighty.

He revealed to me secrets pertaining to His holy angels, and their connection with us.
He revealed to me His love and devotion to those who follow the teachings of King Jesus.

Oh what a privilege and honor-
to behold the mysteries of God, our heavenly Creator and Father.

As an adult, I now remember-
the many heavenly things that were revealed to me, God's sent messenger and daughter.

For as a child, you see-
King Jesus did reveal heavenly things to me.

Although, at the time, I did not fully understand-
that I was placed in, and guided by King Jesus' life-saving hand.

Oh what a glorious honor-
to be known as one of God's sent messengers and daughter.

Holy, holy, holy-
are the mysteries and secrets of God Almighty!!!

THE SPOKEN WORDS THAT *DISPLEASE CHRIST, THE FOREVER-LIVING KING, AND ME*

BARBARA SPEAKING TO CHRIST *JESUS,* THE FOREVER-REIGNING KING

THEY SPEAK THE WORDS, *O LORD KING-*
THAT RELEASE *NO GOOD THING.*

FOR THEIR *SPOKEN WORDS, YOU SEE-*
GO AGAINST THE *REALM OF HOLINESS; CALLED GOD ALMIGHTY.*

AND *THEIR PHYSICAL AND VERBAL ACTIONS, YOU SEE-*
OFFEND *THE GREAT AND HOLY CHRIST ALMIGHTY.*

THEY SPEAK AND KNOW *GOD'S HOLY WORDS, DEAR ONE-*
BUT THEIR LIFE STYLES ARE NOT THAT OF *THE KING'S OBEDIENT AND FAITHFUL DAUGHTER AND SON.*

BARBARA SPEAKING TO GOD'S CHILDREN

DEAR CHILDREN OF *CHRIST, THE FOREVER RULING AND REIGNING KING OF KINGS-*
YOU MUST EXHIBIT, AT ALL TIMES, *GOOD AND HOLY THINGS.*

YOU MUST EXHIBIT *CHRIST JESUS' HOLY WAY-*
AS YOU GO ABOUT YOUR *CHRISTIAN WALK EACH AND EVERY DAY.*

FOR *HOLY AND TRUE-*
IS *THE KING WHO REIGNS AND RULES OVER ME AND YOU.*

HOLY, HOLY, HOLY-
IS THE KING AND GOD ALMIGHTY!!!

I WANT TO HEAR MORE THAN MERE WORDS, SAYS CHRIST JESUS, THE FOREVER-LIVING KING

CHRIST, THE FOREVER-LIVING KING, SPEAKING

I CAN HEAR YOUR UNSPOKEN WORDS, DEAR CHILDREN.
I CAN HEAR THE UNSPOKEN WORDS FROM THOSE OF YOU FROM EVERY NATION.

FOR YOUR WORDS, YOU SEE-
HAVE REACHED THE THRONE OF CHRIST ALMIGHTY.

YOUR SPOKEN WORDS ARE VAIN-
FOR THEY ONLY EXIST WHEN YOUR MIND, BODY AND SOUL EXPERIENCE WORLDLY PAIN.

FOR WHEN YOU SPEAK-
YOUR WORDS DO NOT ENTER THE HOLY REALM OF THE KING WHOM YOU SHOULD SEEK.

YOUR SPOKEN AND UNSPOKEN WORDS ARE MEANINGLESS TO ME.
FOR YOUR ACTIONS DO NOT LIVE UP TO THE VERSION OF HOLINESS THAT IS ACCEPTED BY GOD ALMIGHTY.

I CAN HEAR YOU AS YOU SPEAK OF ME, DEAR ONES.
BUT I WILL NOT ACKNOWLEDGE YOUR PRESENCE, FOR YOU SPEAK MEANINGLESS WORDS THAT COME FROM THE BEINGS OF MY EARTHLY DAUGHTERS AND SONS.

I WILL NOT ACCEPT *MEANINGLESS WORDS THAT COME FROM EARTH'S CHILDREN.*
I WILL NOT ACKNOWLEDGE *THE PRESENCE OF THOSE WHO AREN'T CHOSEN.*

FOR *HOLY AND TRUE-*
IS THE KING AND GOD WHO *DEMANDS OBEDIENCE FROM ALL OF YOU.*

YOU MUST FOLLOW AND ABIDE BY *MY VERSION OF HOLINESS.*
FOR YOU ARE IN THE PRESENCE OF *HE WHO SHARES HIS REALM OF GOODNESS.*

HOLY, HOLY, HOLY-
IS THE KING AND GOD ALMIGHTY!!!

THERE ARE MANY GOD'S, BUT ONLY ONE CREATOR, *SAYS CHRIST JESUS, THE FOREVER-LIVING KING, GOD AND CREATOR*

CHRIST, THE FOREVER-LIVING KING, SPEAKING

DEAR CHILDREN-
FROM EVERY NATION.

YOU CAN MAKE *ANYTHING-*
OR ANYONE, *YOUR GOD OR KING-*

BUT, *YOU CANNOT, YOU SEE-*
CREATE OR SERVE *ANYONE OR THING THAT IS GREATER THAN ME.*

FOR *I, THE LORD GOD-*
AM THE ONLY DIVINE ONE WHO *CREATED YOU OUT OF LOVE.*

BELIEVE ME, *DEAR SON AND DAUGHTER-*
WHEN I TELL YOU THAT *I AM THE ONLY ETERNAL GOD AND CREATOR.*

FOR THERE IS *NO OTHER, YOU SEE-*
WHO IS *YOUR ETERNAL LORD, GOD, AND KING ALMIGHTY.*

FOR *GOD, THE FATHER, AND I-*
FORMED YOU FROM THE DUST OF THE GROUND, *WHICH IS BELOW THE UNENDING SKY.*

FOR *HOLY AND TRUE-*
IS THE GOD AND FATHER WHO CREATED YOU.

YOU MAY SEEK OTHER GODS TO *FULFILL YOUR FANTASY.*
BUT THERE IS ONLY *ONE TRUE GOD ALMIGHTY.*

FOR *GOD, THE FATHER, AND I, YOU SEE-*
RELEASED THE HOLY SPIRIT THAT *SPEAKS THE HOLY WORDS THAT COME FROM GOD, THE FATHER, AND ME; CHRIST ALMIGHTY.*

HOLY, HOLY, HOLY-
IS GOD, THE FATHER; YES, JEHOVAH, THE ALMIGHTY!!!

CHRIST, THE KING, WILL JUDGE AS HE RULES

BARBARA SPEAKING

CHRIST JESUS, *THE EVERLASTING RULER-*
IS *THE FINAL JUDGE AND OUR SAVIOR.*

FOR *CHRIST, THE ETERNAL KING, YOU SEE-*
HAS *THE DIVINE POWER TO SAVE YOU AND ME.*

I WILL BOW *IN THE HOLY PRESENCE OF THE FINAL JUDGE, YOU SEE-*
FOR HE IS *THE ONE WHO DETERMINES MY DESTINY.*

FOR *HOLY AND TRUE-*
IS THE KING WHO WILL *JUDGE ME AND YOU.*

HOLY, HOLY, HOLY-
IS THE FINAL JUDGE CALLED CHRIST ALMIGHTY!!!

AND HE, KING JESUS, WILL JUDGE US ALL

<u>BARBARA SPEAKING</u>

CHRIST JESUS, OUR FOREVER-REIGNING GOD AND KING, WAS GIVEN-
THE DIVINE POWER AND AUTHORITY *TO JUDGE HIS GREATEST CREATION.*

THIS *DIVINE PRIVILEGE AND POWER-*
WAS GIVEN TO *KING* JESUS, BY JEHOVAH, HIS ORIGIN, GOD AND FATHER.

ON THE JUDGMENT DAY-
KING JESUS WILL SEND OUT HIS FINAL DECISION ON THOSE WHO DID AND DID NOT *FOLLOW HIS LIFE REWARDING HOLY WAY.*

FOR *HOLY AND REAL-*
IS THE FINAL DECISION THAT WE WILL ALL FEEL.

FOR *HOLY AND TRUE-*
IS THE KING WHO WILL JUDGE ME AND YOU.

HOLY, HOLY, HOLY-
IS THE ETERNAL JUDGE CALLED CHRIST ALMIGHTY!!!

AS HE SITS ON HIS MIGHTY HEAVENLY THRONE

CHRIST JESUS, THE ETERNAL KING AND JUDGE, SPEAKING

I WILL JUDGE ALL OF YOU-
FOR I AM THE ETERNAL KING, WHO IS FOREVER TRUE.

MY FINAL JUDGMENT IS REAL-
IT IS A DECISION THAT ALL OF MY CREATION WILL FEEL.

FOR HOLY AND TRUE-
IS THE KING WHO WILL JUDGE YOU.

BE AWARE, DEAR CHILDREN-
THAT I AM THE LORD, GOD, AND CREATOR OF EVERY NATION.

BE AWARE, DEAR ONES-
FOR I AM THE FINAL JUDGE OVER MY EARTHLY DAUGHTERS AND SONS.

FOR, FROM MY MIGHTY THRONE IN HEAVEN ABOVE-
I WILL JUDGE THOSE WHOM I TRULY LOVE.

FOR HOLY AND TRUE-
IS THE ETERNAL KING AND GOD WHO RULES AND REIGNS OVER ALL OF YOU.

HOLY, HOLY, HOLY-
IS THE LORD AND GOD CALLED CHRIST ALMIGHTY!!!

YES! I HAD A TALK WITH THE KING THIS MORNING

BARBARA SPEAKING

IT WAS BRIGHT AND EARLY-
THE DAY THAT I HAD A SPIRITUAL TALK WITH MY LORD, GOD AND KING; CHRIST ALMIGHTY.

IT WAS EARLY IN THE MORNING-
WHEN I FELT THE NEED TO COMMUNICATE WITH CHRIST JESUS, MY FOREVER-REIGNING KING.

I SHARED WITH HIM THE CONCERNS OF MY HEART-
FOR I KNEW THAT HIS HOLY PRESENCE WITHIN ME WOULD NEVER DEPART.

OH, HE WAS SO UNDERSTANDING-
HE SPOKE TO MY SPIRIT, AS MY LORD, GOD AND KING.

HE REVEALED TO ME-
THAT HE WOULD TAKE CARE OF THE CONCERNS THAT LINGERED IN THE SOUL OF THE MESSENGER (BARBARA) OF GOD ALMIGHTY.

OH HOW DELIGHTFUL-
TO BE ABLE TO COMMUNICATE WITH THE DIVINE KING WHO IS GRACIOUS AND WONDERFUL.

FOR HIS HOLY SPIRIT DID STAY-
UNTIL THE END OF MY NEVER ENDING DAY.

HOLY, HOLY, HOLY-
IS THE LINGERING SPIRIT OF CHRIST JESUS; THE KING ALMIGHTY!!!

FOR ON THAT *BLESSED MORNING-*
MY EXCITED SPIRIT DID *COMMUNICATE WITH CHRIST JESUS,*
MY ETERNAL GOD AND KING.

HOLY, HOLY, HOLY-
IS MY LOVE FOR CHRIST ALMIGHTY!!!

CHRIST *JESUS, THE FAITHFUL KING AND GOD*

<u>BARBARA SPEAKING</u>

CHRIST JESUS-
IS FAITHFUL AND TRUE TO *BELIEVING US.*

HE HAS GIVEN ME-
EVERYTHING THAT COMES TO *A CHILD OF THE FOREVER-*
LIVING AND REIGNING GOD ALMIGHTY.

FOR HE ANSWERS AND HONORS *MY EVERY PRAYER-*
YES! HE IS A TRUE AND *FAITHFUL GOD AND FATHER.*

OH HOW I ADORE-
THE HEAVENLY KING WHO IS *MY OPEN DOOR.*

HE IS *THE DOOR TO FREEDOM AND EVERLASTING LIFE, YOU SEE-*
FOR HE IS *THE ETERNAL KING-YES! HE IS CHRIST ALMIGHTY.*

HOLY, HOLY, HOLY-
IS THE FAITHFUL KING AND GOD ALMIGHTY!!!

FOR *HE WATCHES OVER US-*
YES! HE REIGNS AND RULES OVER *THE MEEK, THE STRONG,*
AND THE RIGHTEOUS.

HOLY, HOLY, HOLY-
IS THE FOREVER-LIVING KING; CHRIST ALMIGHTY!!!

YOU, O FAITHFUL KING AND GOD, *DID IT AGAIN!!!*

BARBARA SPEAKING

YOU DID IT AGAIN!
YES, YOU, *KING JESUS; MY GOD AND FAITHFUL FRIEND!*

I DID NOT *DOUBT, NOR WORRY-*
I WAITED PATIENTLY ON *THE KING ALMIGHTY.*

I WAITED PATIENTLY, *YOU SEE-*
FOR MY PRAYERS TO BE *HEARD AND HONORED BY GOD ALMIGHTY.*

IT DID NOT TAKE LONG-
FOR HE HONORED MY SPIRITUAL REQUEST *AS I SANG TO HIM A PRAISING SONG.*

I WAS *VERY EXCITED, YOU SEE-*
TO WITNESS *THE FULFILLMENT OF THE REQUEST THAT MY SPIRIT WHISPERED TO THE KING ALMIGHTY.*

I GIVE YOU PRAISE-
DURING THESE *PRAISE WORTHY DAYS!*

HALLELUJAH! HALLELUJAH! HALLELUJAH-
TO THE ETERNAL KING AND *ONLY BEGOTTEN SON OF GOD, THE FATHER,* JEHOVAH!!!

IN THE *BEGINNING*

BARBARA SPEAKING

IN THE BEGINNING, YOU SEE-
EXISTED *THE HOLY WORKS OF THE KING ALMIGHTY.*

IN THE BEGINNING-
EXISTED *THE HOLINESS OF GOD ALMIGHTY.*

FOR, *IN THE BEGINNING-*
EXISTED OUR CREATOR AND GOD, *THE FOREVER REIGNING CHRIST, THE KING.*

FOR, *IN THE BEGINNING OF HUMAN LIFE-*
GOD CREATED ADAM AND EVE, THE *FIRST HUSBAND AND WIFE.*

FOR *ADAM AND EVE, YOU SEE-*
WERE FORMED FROM THE DUST OF THE GROUND, BY *GOD, THE FATHER, AND JESUS CHRIST, THE REIGNING SON OF JEHOVAH, THE ALMIGHTY.*

OUT OF *DIVINE LOVE, YOU SEE-*
ALMIGHTY GOD CREATED YOU AND ME.

FOR IN THE VERY BEGINNING OF *HUMAN LIFE AND TIME, YOU SEE-*
EXISTED *CHRIST, THE SAVIOR, AND GOD, THE FATHER ALMIGHTY.*

FOR *HOLY AND TRUE-*
IS THE EXISTING KING THAT *FORMED HUMAN TIME, AND ME AND YOU.*

HOLY, HOLY, HOLY-
IS THE BEGINNING OF TIME AND LIFE THAT WAS BROUGHT INTO EXISTENCE BY GOD ALMIGHTY!!!

FOR *IN THE BEGINNING-*
EXISTENCE BEHELD *THE HOLY PRESENCE OF CHRIST ALMIGHTY.*

HOLY, HOLY, HOLY AND TRUE-
IS THE EXISTING GOD WHO CREATED ME AND YOU!!!

BELIEVE! BELIEVE! BELIEVE! BELIEVE IN ME, *SAYS CHRIST JESUS, THE HEAVEN SENT KING ALMIGHTY!!!*

<u>THE HEAVEN SENT KING, CHRIST ALMIGHTY, SPEAKING</u>

DEAR CHILDREN-
YES! YOU FROM EVERY NATION!

BELIEVE! BELIEVE! BELIEVE!
BELIEVE IN THE HOLY HEAVEN DESCENDED MESSAGES THAT YOU RECEIVE.

FOR I, YOUR HEAVEN SENT GOD AND KING-
HAS SENT YOU A WONDERFUL, GREAT, AND HOLY THING.

BELIEVE IN MY WONDERS-
THAT I REVEAL TO MY EARTHLY SONS AND DAUGHTERS.

BELIEVE IN LIFE EVERLASTING-
BELIEVE! BELIEVE! BELIEVE! DEAR CHILDREN: BELIEVE IN CHRIST JESUS, YOUR HOLY HEAVEN SENT GOD AND KING

FOR I TRULY EXIST-
MY HOLY SPIRIT AND PRESENCE MOVES IN YOUR BLESSED MIDST.

FOR YOUR HOLY EXISTING KING, YOU SEE-
TRULY LOVES THOSE WHO ARE CALLED AND CHOSEN BY ME.

HOLY, HOLY, HOLY-
IS THE FOREVER LOVING KING, CHRIST ALMIGHTY!!!

BELIEVE IN ME, FOR I AM THE MIGHTY ONE.
BELIEVE IN ME, FOR I AM GOD, THE FATHER'S, ONLY BEGOTTEN SON.

FOR HOLY AND TRUE-
IS THE MIGHTY KING WHO WAS SENT FROM SWEET HEAVEN BY GOD, THE FATHER, TO DIE ON MY HOLY CROSS OF LOVE FOR BELOVED AND BLESSED YOU.

HOLY, HOLY, HOLY-
IS CHRIST, THE HEAVEN SENT KING AND GOD ALMIGHTY!!!

MY DIVINE ASSIGNMENT OF LOVE

BARBARA SPEAKING

OUT OF OBEDIENCE TO *JEHOVAH* GOD, OUR HEAVENLY FATHER- CHRIST *JESUS,* THE FOREVER REIGNING KING, *SHARES MY HEAVEN ORDERED ASSIGNMENT OF LOVE, WITH ME, HIS FAITHFUL FRIEND AND TRUST WORTHY DAUGHTER.*

HOLD ME, O GREAT AND HOLY KING *JESUS-*
CLING TO ME WITH THE DIVINE STRENGTH THAT GOD, OUR FATHER, HAS GIVEN US.

WALK WITH ME-
THROUGH *THIS SPIRITUAL TRAGEDY.*

FOR THE *BATTLE HAS BEGUN-*
AND THE REALM OF EVIL *HAS TAKEN DOWN YOUR VULNERABLE DAUGHTER AND SON.*

HELP ME *DELIVER OUR HEAVENLY FATHER'S HOLY PRESENCE TODAY-*
AS YOU AND I *LEAD THEM TO YOUR LIFE REWARDING HOLY WAY.*

FOR *HOLY, ETERNAL AND TRUE-*
IS THE HEAVENLY GOD AND FATHER WHO *SENDS TO HIS EARTHLY LOVED ONES, ME AND YOU.*

HOLY, HOLY, HOLY-
IS KING JESUS, THE ONLY BEGOTTEN SON OF JEHOVAH GOD, THE FATHER, ALMIGHTY!!!

MY DIVINE ASSIGNMENT AT A HOSPITAL IN DELAWARE COUNTY

<u>BARBARA SPEAKING</u>

CHRIST JESUS, THE FOREVER-LIVING KING, YOU SEE-
SENT ME TO A HOSPITAL IN DELAWARE COUNTY, TO SHARE HIS HOLY PRESENCE AND SPIRITUAL VISIBILITY.

FOR THROUGH ME, THE KING'S SENT MESSENGER-
I WAS ABLE TO SPEAK TO HIS CALLED AND CHOSEN SON AND DAUGHTER.

FOR OUT OF DIVINE LOVE FOR US-
I WAS GRANTED THE ASSIGNMENT TO REVEAL THE HOLY PRESENCE OF KING JESUS.

FOR HOLY AND REAL-
IS THE PRESENCE OF CHRIST, THE KING, THAT HIS CHILDREN, THROUGH ME, DID SEE AND FEEL.

AS AN ADMITTED PATIENT, YOU SEE-
I GAIN PHYSICAL ACCESS TO THE LOVED ONES OF GOD ALMIGHTY.

EVERYONE WAS KIND TO ME-
FOR THEY FELT THE HOLY PRESENCE OF CHRIST JESUS, THE KING ALMIGHTY.

FOR *HOLY AND TRUE-*
IS THE KING WHO *BROUGHT MY WEAK BODY AND ASSIGNMENT OF GODLY LOVE THROUGH.*

HOLY, HOLY, HOLY-
IS THE ASSIGNMENT OF LOVE THAT DESCENDED TO THE CHILDREN OF GOD ALMIGHTY!!!

MY NEEDED IV (INTRAVENOUS)

BARBARA SPEAKING TO CHRIST JESUS, THE HEAVEN SENT KING

O HOLY KING-
YOU HAVE GIVEN ME AN ASSIGNMENT WHICH INCLUDES A HEAVEN SENT GLORIOUS THING.

FOR THROUGH ME-
ONE OF THE MESSENGERS OF GOD ALMIGHTY-
WAS REVEALED, YOUR VISIBILITY.

YOU PERMITTED ME-
TO SHARE YOUR HOLY PRESENCE AND SPIRIT WITH THE LOVED ONES OF CHRIST JESUS, THE HEAVENLY KING ALMIGHTY.

OUT OF GREAT DIVINE LOVE, YOU SEE-
YOU SENT ME TO YOUR CHILDREN (THE STAFF) AT A HOSPITAL IN DELAWARE COUNTY, WHO ARE CALLED AND LOVED BY THE KING ALMIGHTY.

AS A PATIENT THERE-
THE STAFF WAS ABLE, THROUGH ME, TO FEEL THE HOLY PRESENCE OF THE KING WHO WAS NEAR.

HOLY, HOLY, HOLY-
IS THE VISIBLE PRESENCE OF GOD, THE KING ALMIGHTY!!!

THROUGH AN IV-
I REGAINED THE STRENGTH THAT HAD PREVIOUSLY LEFT ME.

THE IV SOLUTION-
GAVE ME THE STRENGTH TO SPEAK TO GOD'S GREATEST CREATION.

FOR OUT OF DIVINE LOVE-
WE ALL WERE CREATED FROM THE DUST OF THE GROUND, BY GOD, THE FATHER, AND KING JESUS, HIS ONLY BEGOTTEN SON, WHO DWELLS WITH HIM IN SWEET HEAVEN ABOVE.

OUT OF DIVINE LOVE-
GOD, THE HOLY HEAVENLY FATHER, SENT ME TO THE HOSPITAL WITH THE GIFT OF HIS HOLY PRESENCE, WHICH DESCENDS TO US FROM HEAVEN ABOVE.

HOLY, HOLY, HOLY-
WAS MY ASSIGNMENT FROM GOD, THE HEAVENLY KING ALMIGHTY!!!

MY WOUNDS; MY HEAVEN APPROVED WOUNDS

BARBARA SPEAKING

AS A PATIENT IN THE HOSPITAL TODAY-
I BEAR MY GOD ORDERED AND APPROVED WOUNDS THAT LEAD TO CHRIST, THE KING'S, HOLY LIFE REWARDING WAY.

FOR, THE NURSES, YOU SEE-
PUT IN MY HAND AND ARM A WELL NEEDED IV.

FOR *CHRIST JESUS SENT ME-*
TO A SPECIFIC HOSPITAL, TO *SHARE HIS HOLY WORDS AND PRESENCE WITH THE LOVED ONES OF GOD ALMIGHTY.*

FOR *HOLY AND TRUE-*
IS THE KING WHO HAS *SENT ME TO WELL-LOVED YOU.*

HE HAS SENT ME-
TO *REVEAL HIS DIVINITY.*

FOR *KING JESUS-*
HAS SACRIFICED HIS PRECIOUS BELOVED BODY FOR ALL OF US.

HOLY, HOLY, HOLY-
IS THE SACRIFICIAL ACT OF GOD ALMIGHTY!!!

FOR *HE MOVES, YOU SEE-*
IN THE MIDST OF THE MEDICAL STAFF AND HOSPITAL WORKERS *WHO ARE LOVE BY FOREVER-REIGNING HE.*

HOLY, HOLY, HOLY-
IS MY KING AND GOD ALMIGHTY!!!

FOR *HE HAS SENT ME, YOU SEE-*
TO DO *A GREAT WORK FOR HOLY HE.*

FOR *MY DIVINE ASSIGNMENT OF LOVE-*
WAS SENT TO ME *FROM SWEET HEAVEN ABOVE.*

I WILL ENDURE, YOU SEE-
THE TEMPORARY PAIN THAT WAS APPROVED AND APPRECIATED BY THE HEAVENLY KING ALMIGHTY.

HOLY, HOLY, HOLY-
ARE THE WOUNDS THAT I BEAR FOR THE SAKE OF THE LOVED ONES OF GOD ALMIGHTY!!!

MY VISIBLE AND SPIRITUAL WOUNDS: REPRESENT MY LOVE FOR CHRIST, THE FOREVER-LIVING AND REIGNING KING; AND MY GOD

BARBARA SPEAKING

THE SPIRITUAL AND PHYSICAL WOUNDS THAT I CONSTANTLY BEAR-
REVEAL THE LOVE THAT MY HEAVENLY KING AND I SHARE.

FOR THE WOUNDS THAT I BEAR, YOU SEE-
IS DONE OUT OF MY LOVE FOR MY BELOVED KING; THE FOREVER-LIVING CHRIST ALMIGHTY.

FOR HOLY AND TRUE-
IS OUR (KING JESUS AND BARBARA) LOVE FOR WORTHY YOU.

FOR KING JESUS, YOU SEE-
SENT ME TO HIS CALLED LOVED ONES AT A HOSPITAL IN DARBY.

THE WOUNDS THAT WERE PLACED UPON MY SPIRIT AND BODY-
REVEAL MY DEVOTION TO MY FAITHFUL KING AND GOD ALMIGHTY.

FOR HOLY AND TRUE-
IS THE HEAVENLY KING WHO SEES ALL OF HIS SENT MESSENGERS AND PROPHETS THROUGH.

THEREFORE, *I WILL BEAR WITH GLADNESS-*
THE WOUNDS THAT *REVEALS CHRIST, THE FOREVER-LIVING KING'S FAITHFULNESS.*

FOR *HOLY, HOLY, HOLY-*
IS THE *FAITHFUL KING AND GOD ALMIGHTY!!!*

MY ASSIGNMENT OF DIVINE LOVE-
DESCENDED INTO MY REALM OF OBEDIENCE, *FROM SWEET HEAVEN ABOVE.*

HOLY, HOLY, HOLY-
ARE THE HEAVEN SENT ASSIGNMENTS OF GOD *ALMIGHTY!!!*

WHEN THE PRECIOUS *WOUNDS OF CHRIST JESUS CALL OUT TO ME, I BOW*

BARBARA SPEAKING

I CAN HEAR-
THE HOLY WOUNDS OF *CHRIST, THE KING, THAT ARE VERY NEAR.*

I CAN HEAR *THE LIFE SAVING SOUND-*
OF THE GOD WHO IS *ALWAYS AROUND.*

FOR *HIS HOLY WOUNDS, YOU SEE-*
CALL OUT TO BLESSED ME.

I BOW, YOU SEE-
IN THE MIDST OF *THE KING'S HOLY LIFE SAVING WOUNDS OF DIVINE LOVE THAT CALL OUT TO ME.*

FOR *KING JESUS' HOLY WOUNDS, YOU SEE-*
BECKON TO *BELIEVING YOU AND ME.*

FOR *HOLY AND TRUE-*
ARE THE WOUNDS THAT *EXIST FOR ME AND YOU.*

HOLY, HOLY, HOLY-
ARE THE LIVING WOUNDS OF CHRIST ALMIGHTY!!!

MY BLESSED SPIRIT AND SOUL *BOW IN THE MIDST OF THE KING'S DIVINE WOUNDS, YOU SEE-*
FOR HIS HOLY WOUNDS ARE *THE PHYSICAL PRESENCE OF HIS LOVE FOR YOU AND ME.*

HOLY, HOLY, HOLY-
ARE THE WOUNDS OF THE KING ALMIGHTY!!!

FOR *IN HIS PRECIOUS BODY-*
ARE THE BARING *WOUNDS OF CHRIST ALMIGHTY.*

I WILL CLING TO HIS HOLY WOUNDS *WITH DIVINE LOVE-*
AS I WORSHIP *THE KING WHO DESCENDED FROM SWEET HEAVEN ABOVE.*

HOLY AND TRUE-
ARE THE WOUNDS OF THE KING THAT *EXIST FOR ME AND YOU.*

MY SPIRITUAL, PHYSICAL, AND EMOTIONAL STRENGTH, *COME FROM YOU, O MIGHTY KING JESUS*

<u>BARBARA SPEAKING TO KING JESUS</u>

O LORD JESUS-
YOU ARE *THE HOLY ONE WHO CAME TO SAVE US.*

You are my everything-
You are my strength; yes, my holy God and King.

For knowing You, *King Jesus-*
gives me the strength *to seek the beloved children of almighty God; the righteous.*

For You, *King Jesus, are the righteous one-*
who has been *sent by God, the Father, to save His sinking daughter and son.*

Oh how *I truly adore-*
the holy God and King, whom *I will look for no more.*

For You, O blessed King, *in You, I have found-*
a loving and earthly God *who is always around*

For *holy and true-*
is the heaven sent love called You.

Holy, holy, holy-
is my strength that comes from Christ almighty!!!

For you are *my divine rock of love-*
that descended to your earthly children *from sweet heaven above.*

For *holy, eternal and true-*

is the heaven sent strength that *comes from beloved and blessed You.*

CHRIST JESUS SENT WOUNDED ME

BARBARA SPEAKING

Christ, the forever-reigning King-
sent me to perform a wonderful heavenly thing.

For he sent, you see-
blessed wounded me.

For my wounds of love-
exhibited God's mercy that descended to us from sweet Heaven above.

My "spiritual and physical" wounds, you see-
represent the love and devotion that come from God Almighty.

For my "wounds of joy"-
were sent to speak to the King's called girl and boy.

For holy and true-
were the words that were given to blessed you.

Holy, holy, holy-
are the "wounds" that are on the body of the sent messenger (Barbara) of Christ Almighty!!!

THE MANY WOUNDS THAT YOU BORE FOR US, *O GREAT AND HOLY* KING JESUS

<u>BARBARA SPEAKING TO KING JESUS</u>

I WILL SNUGGLE AND BATHE *IN THE HOLY WOUNDS THAT YOU BORE FOR US.*
I WILL TAKE COMFORT IN *THE SACRIFICIAL ACT OF CHRIST JESUS.*

FOR *YOU BORE FOR US-*
THE WOUNDS THAT WILL *SAVE THE FAITHFUL AND THE RIGHTEOUS.*

MY BLESSED SPIRIT BOWS IN THE MIDST OF *YOUR SPIRITUAL WOUNDS, MY DIVINE LORD, KING AND GOD.*
I SEEK REFUGE IN *THE HOLY ETERNAL KING AND GOD WHOM I WILL ALWAYS LOVE.*

FOR *HOLY AND TRUE-*
ARE THE WOUNDS THAT *COVER THE BODY OF HE WHO SAVES ME AND YOU.*

JESUS CHRIST, THE FOREVER REIGNING KING, *IS THE REALM OF UNENDING HOPE AGAINST VISIBLE HOPE*

<u>CHRIST, THE FOREVER REIGNING KING, SPEAKING</u>

DEAR CHILDREN-
MY CHILDREN OF DESPAIR *FROM EVERY NATION.*

I AM YOUR *FOREVER-LIVING REALM OF HOPE, YOU SEE-*
WHEN YOU EXPERIENCE *THE LOSS OF HOPE THAT DWELLS AMONG THE CHILDREN OF CHRIST ALMIGHTY.*

I AM THE LIVING DOOR, YOU SEE-
AND THE REALM OF DESPAIR *CAN NEVER ENTER THROUGH ME.*

TRUST-
DEAR CHILDREN OF *CHRIST, THE KING, IS A MUST.*

FOR *YOU MUST TRUST IN ME-*
FOR I AM THE ONLY KING WHO CAN *REMOVE THE REALM OF "NO HOPE", AND REPLACE IT WITH THE GIFTS AND PROMISES OF CHRIST ALMIGHTY.*

FOR *HOLY AND REAL-*
IS THE REALM OF HOPE IN ME THAT *MY TRUSTING CHILDREN CAN TRULY FEEL.*

FOR *HOLY AND TRUE-*
IS THE FOREVER-LIVING KING WHO *GIVES DIVINE HOPE AND TRUST TO YOU.*

TRUST IN ME-
FOR I AM THE REALM OF HOPE WHO *SETS MY CHILDREN OF DESPAIR (THE LOSS OF HOPE) FREE.*

HOLY, HOLY, HOLY-
IS THE REALM OF UNENDING HOPE CALLED CHRIST ALMIGHTY!!!

CHRIST, THE FOREVER-LIVING KING'S, GOOD NEWS HAVE ENTERED THE CHOSEN HOSPITAL. *HALLELUJAH!!!*

BARBARA SPEAKING

HALLELUJAH! HALLELUJAH! HALLELUJAH, TO THE ONLY BEGOTTEN SON OF ALMIGHTY GOD, *JEHOVAH!!!*

FOR *KING JESUS,* YOU SEE-
IS *THE ONLY SON WHO CAME FROM THE ETERNAL EXISTENCE OF JEHOVAH GOD, THE ALMIGHTY.*

IT HAS ENTERED, YOU SEE-
THE HOSPITAL THAT WAS *CHOSEN BY THE LOVE AND HOLY PRESENCE OF CHRIST JESUS, THE KING ALMIGHTY.*

FOR *KING JESUS,* YOU SEE-
SENT TO HIS LOVED ONES, *OBEDIENT ME.*

FOR, AS AN *OBEDIENT SERVANT AND MESSENGER OF ALMIGHTY GOD-*
MY DIVINE ASSIGNMENT WAS *TO DELIVER HIS EXPRESSION OF VISIBLE LOVE.*

FOR *HOLY AND REAL-*
IS THE KING'S MESSENGER *(BARBARA)* THAT *THE HOSPITAL STAFF DID SEE, HEAR AND FEEL.*

THROUGH ME-
EVERYONE WITNESSED AND EXPERIENCED *THE HOLY PRESENCE OF GOD ALMIGHTY.*

CHRIST JESUS SENT WOUNDED ME

BARBARA SPEAKING

Christ, the forever-reigning King-
Sent me to perform a wonderful heavenly thing.

For He sent, you see-
Blessed wounded me.

For my wounds of love-
Exhibited God's mercy that descended to us from sweet Heaven above.

My "spiritual and physical" wounds, you see-
Represent the love and devotion that come from God Almighty.

For my "wounds of joy"-
Were sent to speak to the King's called girl and boy.

For holy and true-
Were the words that were given to blessed you.

Holy, holy, holy-
Is the sent messenger (Barbara) of the King Almighty!!!

I HAVE SPOKEN TO YOUR LOVED ONES AT THE HOSPITAL, O GREAT AND HOLY KING JESUS

<u>BARBARA SPEAKING TO CHRIST JESUS, THE GREAT AND HOLY KING</u>

DEAR LORD AND GOD-
I HAVE SPOKEN YOUR HOLY WORDS *TO THOSE WHOM YOU LOVE.*

I HAVE SPOKEN, YOU SEE-
THE HOLY WORDS THAT *YOU HAVE GIVEN TO ME.*

FOR *HOLY AND REAL-*
IS THE MESSENGER *(BARBARA)* WHOM *YOUR LOVED ONES DID SEE AND FEEL.*

HOLY, HOLY, HOLY-
IS THE SENT MESSENGER AND SERVANT *(BARBARA) OF GOD ALMIGHTY!!!*

FOR THE SAKE OF *THE* KING'S *GOOD NEWS*

<u>BARBARA SPEAKING</u>

FOR *THE SAKE OF CHRIST, THE KING'S, GOOD NEWS-*
I WILL GO TO *THOSE WHO DO NOT SIT IN GOD'S CHURCH PEWS.*

FOR *HIS GOOD NEWS, YOU SEE-*
ARE THE LIFE REWARDING WORDS OF GOD ALMIGHTY.

I WILL SPEAK-
TO THOSE WHOM *KING* JESUS *DOES SEEK.*

FOR *HIS HOLY WORDS, YOU SEE-*
ARE SPOKEN TO SENT ME.

HOLY, HOLY, HOLY AND TRUE-
IS THE GOOD NEWS FROM HEAVEN THAT *CHRIST, THE FOREVER-LIVING KING, BRINGS TO ALL OF YOU!!!*

HOLY, HOLY, HOLY-
IS THE GOOD NEWS OF CHRIST ALMIGHTY!!!

CHRIST *JESUS,* THE GRACIOUS FOREVER-REIGNING KING, *WELCOMES HIS LOVED ONES TODAY*

<u>CHRIST *JESUS,* THE FOREVER-REIGNING KING, SPEAKING TO HIS LOVED ONES TODAY</u>

WELCOME! WELCOME! *WELCOME, O BLESSED CHILDREN!*
WELCOME, *MY BELOVED ONES FROM EVERY NATION.*

FOR *I, YOUR LORD, KING AND GOD-*
WELCOME ALL OF YOU *INTO MY UNENDING REALM OF DIVINE LOVE-*

FOR *I AM COMING TO YOU TODAY-*
AS BARBARA, MY SENT MESSENGER, *LEADS YOU THROUGH THE DOOR OF MY HOLY LIFE REWARDING WAY.*

WELCOME, DEAR ONES!
ENTER MY REALM OF EXCITEMENT AND JOY, *O BELOVED DAUGHTERS AND SONS.*

REMEMBER, THAT I, *YOUR LORD, GOD AND SAVIOR, AM ALWAYS NEAR.*
I AM THE HOLY KING WHO DOES CARE.

ENTER! ENTER! ENTER!
ENTER MY HOLY REALM TODAY, *O BLESSED SON AND DAUGHTER!*

FOR *HOLY AND TRUE-*
IS *THE KING WHO WELCOMES YOU.*

HOLY, HOLY, HOLY-
IS *CHRIST JESUS, THE KING ALMIGHTY!!!*

BARBARA WITH GOD'S BLESSED AND BEAUTIFUL DAUGHTER, DR. NITHYA RAMESH, MD: INTERNAL MEDICINE RESIDENT. I THANK YOU, DEAR DOCTOR, FOR YOUR KINDNESS AND PATIENCE DURING MY STAY AT THE HOSPITAL. GOD'S MANY BLESSINGS TO YOU AND YOUR LOVED ONES.

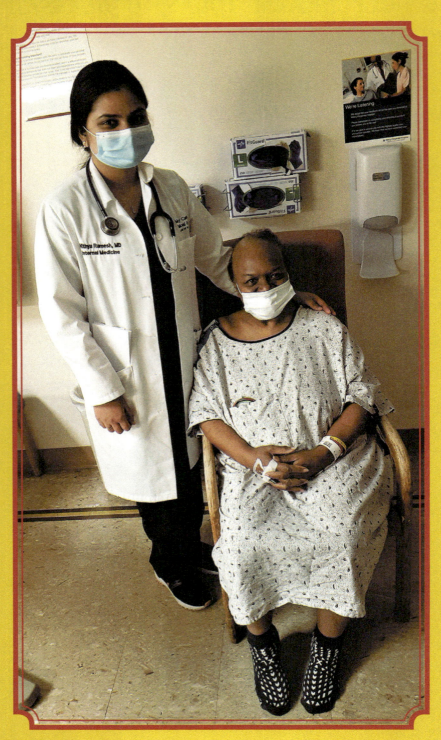

BARBARA WITH THE KING'S DAUGHTER, BEAUTIFUL PATRICIA PHILLIPS FROM ENVIRONMENTAL SERVICES. I THANK YOU DEAR SISTER IN CHRIST JESUS, FOR YOUR KINDNESS DURING MY STAY AT THE HOSPITAL

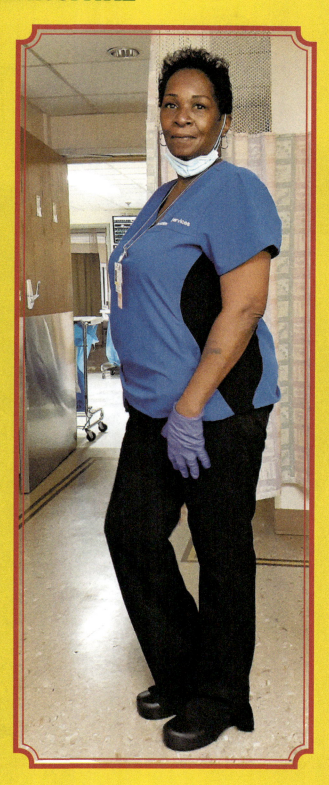

BARBARA WITH THE LOVELY NURSE MICHELLE, GOD'S BLESSED DAUGHTER

BARBARA AND THE PATIENT AND LOVELY NURSE THERESE SNYDER, THE DAUGHTER OF CHRIST, THE FOREVER-LIVING KING OF KINGS. THERESE WAS ONE OF MY BEAUTIFUL NURSES DURING MY STAY AT THE HOSPITAL. GOD'S MANY BLESSINGS TO THERESE AND HER LOVED ONES.

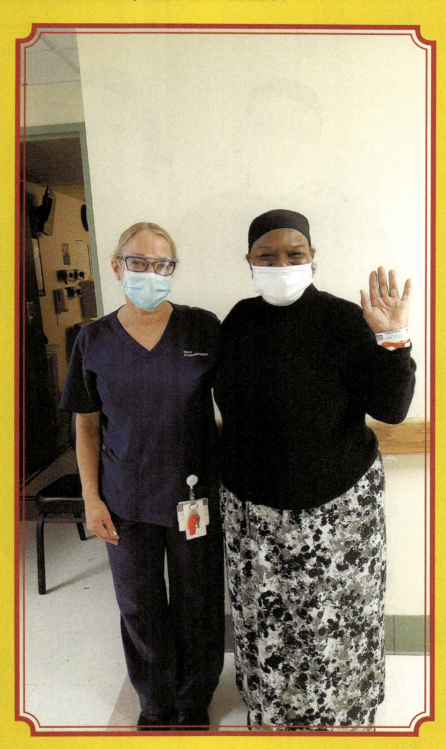

BARBARA AND GOD'S BLESSED AND BELOVED LITTLE GIRL, SANDRA WILLIAMS. THANK YOU VERY MUCH FOR YOUR KINDNESS DURING MY STAY AT THE HOSPITAL. YOU ARE A WONDERFUL ASSET TO THE NURSING DEPARTMENT. ENJOY YOUR GOD GIVEN GIFTS, DEAR SISTER IN CHRIST *JESUS*

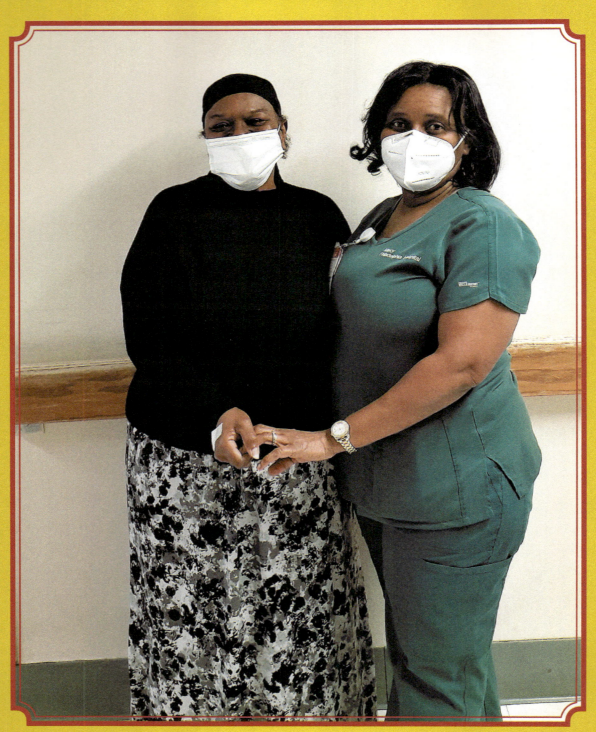

BARBARA WITH GOD'S BELOVED DAUGHTER, THE BEAUTIFUL LORETTA KINES. LORETTA TRANSPORTED ME FROM THE EMERGENCY ROOM TO MY IN PATIENT ROOM. GOD BLESS LORETTA, HER HUSBAND JOHN, AND THEIR TWO PRECIOUS KITTIES

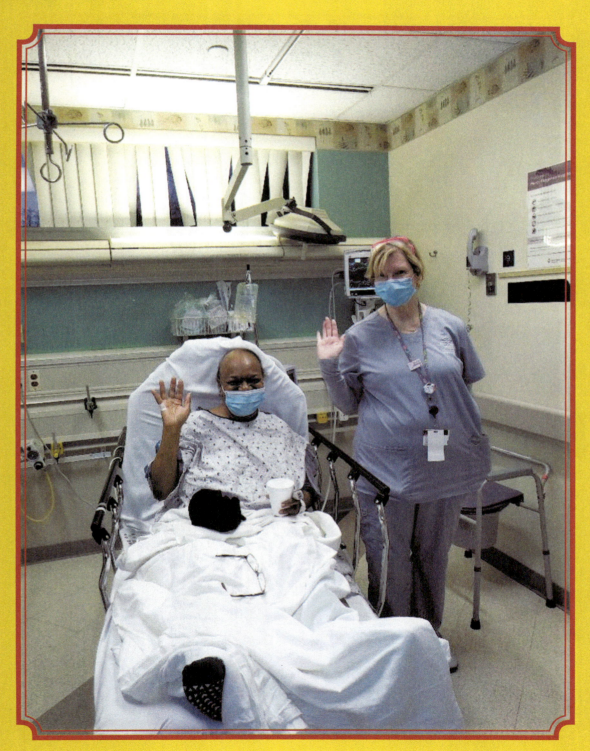

BARBARA WITH GOD'S BELOVED SON DR. SHARMA.

HE WAS VERY PLEASANT AND SOCIABLE DURING MY STAY IN THE EMERGENCY ROOM. A WONDERFUL DOCTOR. GOD'S MANY BLESSINGS TO DR. SHARMA AND HIS LOVED ONES

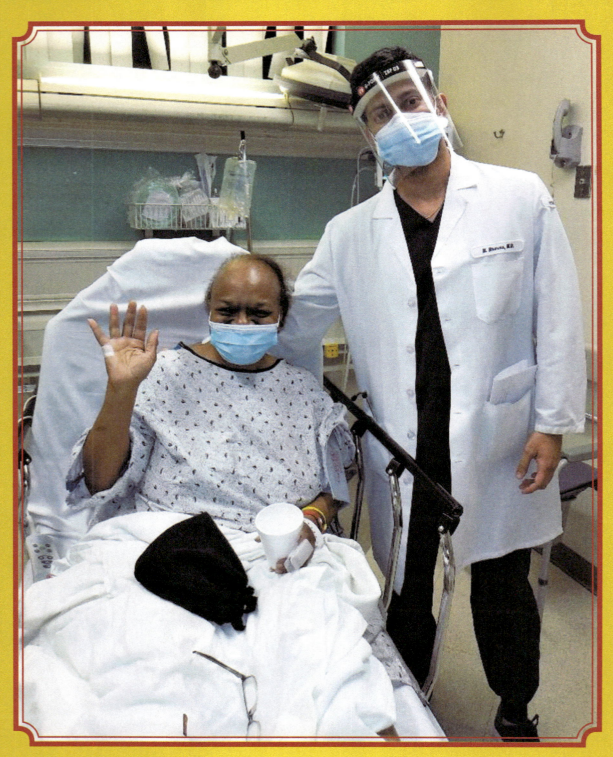

FOUR DAYS AFTER I WAS DISCHARGED FROM THE HOSPITAL, I WAS SCHEDULED FOR AN ULTRASOUND AT THE SAME HOSPITAL. THE LORD GOD WANTED ME TO SHARE HIS HOLY PRESENCE WITH HIS CHILDREN IN THE XRAY DEPARTMENT ALSO. THERE, I MET BEAUTIFUL LISA, WHO PERFORMED THE NECESSARY ULTRASOUND. THANK YOU LISA

I WILL CONTINUE ON MY JOURNEY INTO THE GREAT AND HOLY KING'S REALM OF UNENDING DIVINE LOVE AND HEAVENLY BLISS-*HALLELUJAH!!!*

AS HE SITS ON *HIS MIGHTY HEAVENLY THRONE*

CHRIST *JESUS,* THE ETERNAL *KING* AND JUDGE, SPEAKING

I WILL JUDGE ALL OF YOU-
FOR *I AM THE ETERNAL KING, WHO IS FOREVER TRUE.*

MY FINAL JUDGMENT IS REAL-
IT IS A DECISION THAT *ALL OF MY CREATION WILL FEEL.*

FOR *HOLY AND TRUE-*
IS *THE KING WHO WILL JUDGE YOU.*

BE AWARE, DEAR CHILDREN-
THAT *I AM THE LORD, GOD, AND CREATOR OF EVERY NATION.*

BE AWARE, DEAR ONES-
FOR *I AM THE FINAL JUDGE OVER MY EARTHLY DAUGHTERS AND SONS.*

FOR, FROM *MY MIGHTY THRONE IN HEAVEN ABOVE-*
I WILL JUDGE THOSE WHOM I TRULY LOVE.

FOR *HOLY AND TRUE-*
IS THE ETERNAL *KING AND GOD WHO RULES AND REIGNS OVER ALL OF YOU.*
HOLY, HOLY, HOLY-
IS THE LORD AND GOD CALLED CHRIST ALMIGHTY!!!

MY OTHER PUBLISHED BOOKS

1. WORDS OF INSPIRATION
2. FATHER, ARE YOU CALLING ME? *(CHILDREN'S BOOK)*
3. DAUGHTER OF COURAGE
4. A HOUSE DIVIDED CANNOT STAND
5. TASTE AND SEE THE GOODNESS OF THE LORD
6. HUMILITY- THE COST OF DISCIPLESHIP
7. WILL YOU BE MY BRIDE FIRST?
8. ODE TO MY BELOVED
9. FATHER, THEY KNOW NOT WHAT THEY DO
10. IN MY FATHER'S HOUSE *(CHILDREN'S BOOK)*
11. IN MY GARDEN *(CHILDREN'S BOOK)*
12. THE BATTLE IS OVER
13. THE GOSPEL ACCORDING TO THE LAMB'S BRIDE
14. THE PRESENT TESTAMENT
15. THE PRESENT TESTAMENT VOL. 2
16. THE PRESENT TESTAMENT VOL. 3
17. THE PRESENT TESTAMENT VOL. 4
18. THE PRESENT TESTAMENT VOL. 5
19. THE PRESENT TESTAMENT VOL. 6
20. THE PRESENT TESTAMENT VOL. 7
21. THE PRESENT TESTAMENT VOL. 8
22. THE PRESENT TESTAMENT VOL. 9
23. THE PRESENT TESTAMENT VOL. 10

24. THE PRESENT TESTAMENT VOL. 11
25. THE PRESENT TESTAMENT VOL. 12
26. THE PRESENT TESTAMENT VOL. 13
27. THE PRESENT TESTAMENT VOL. 14
28. THE PRESENT TESTAMENT VOL. 15
29. THE PRESENT TESTAMENT VOL. 16
30. THE PRESENT TESTAMENT VOL. 17
31. BEHOLD THE PRESENT TESTAMENT "VOLUMES 18, 19, 20, 21, 22 AND 23"
32. BEHOLD MY PRESENT TESTAMENT "VOLUMES 24 AND 25"
33. BEHOLD MY PRESENT TESTAMENT "VOLUMES 26, 27, 28 AND 29"
34. BEHOLD MY PRESENT TESTAMENT "VOLUMES 30, 31 AND 32"
35. BEHOLD MY PRESENT TESTAMENT "VOLUMES 33 AND 34"
36. BEHOLD MY PRESENT TESTAMENT "VOLUMES 35, 36 AND 37"
37. BEHOLD MY PRESENT TESTAMENT "VOLUMES 38 & 39"
38. BEHOLD MY PRESENT TESTAMENT "VOLUMES 40 & 41"
39. BEHOLD MY PRESENT TESTAMENT "VOLUMES 42 & 43"
40. BEHOLD MY PRESENT TESTAMENT "VOLUMES 44 & 45"
41. BEHOLD MY PRESENT TESTAMENT "VOLUME 46"
42. BEHOLD MY PRESENT TESTAMENT "VOLUMES 47 & 48"
43. BEHOLD MY PRESENT TESTAMENT "VOLUMES 49 & 50"
44. BEHOLD MY PRESENT TESTAMENT "VOLUME 51"
45. LET THERE BE *LOVE—CHILDREN'S BOOK*

46. BEHOLD MY PRESENT TESTAMENT: *"A NEW BIRTH - VOLUMES 52-56"*
47. BEHOLD MY PRESENT TESTAMENT, VOLUME 57 *JESUS: KING* OF PEACE
48. BEHOLD MY PRESENT TESTAMENT, VOLUME 58 AND 59 "TO BE SURROUNDED BY ALMIGHTY GOD, THE BLESSED AND HOLY TRINITY"
49. *HASHEM/JEHOVAH/YAHWEH:* ALMIGHTY GOD, THE FATHER
50. I EXIST, *SAYS ALMIGHTY GOD*

9781665547598